WAKING UP FROM THE AMERICAN DREAM

by

GREGORY HOOD

FOREWORD BY KEVIN MACDONALD

Counter-Currents Publishing Ltd.
San Francisco
2016

Cover image by Nathan Malone

Cover design by Kevin I. Slaughter

Published in the United States by
COUNTER-CURRENTS PUBLISHING LTD.
P.O. Box 22638
San Francisco, CA 94122
USA
http://www.counter-currents.com/

Hardcover ISBN: 978-1-940933-26-9
Paperback ISBN: 978-1-940933-27-6
E-book ISBN: 978-1-940933-28-3

Library of Congress Cataloging-in-Publication Data

Names: Hood, Gregory, 1980- author.
Title: Waking up from the American dream / by Gregory Hood.
Description: San Francisco : Counter-Currents Publishing, Ltd., [2016] |
    Includes bibliographical references and index.
Identifiers: LCCN 2016008590 (print) | LCCN 2016020764 (ebook) | ISBN
    9781940933269 (hardcover : alk. paper) | ISBN 9781940933276 (pbk. : alk.
    paper) | ISBN 9781940933283 (E-book)
Subjects: LCSH: Conservatism--United States. | White nationalism--United
    States. | United States--Politics and government--21st century.
Classification: LCC JC573.2.U6 H658 2016 (print) | LCC JC573.2.U6 (ebook) |
    DDC 320.540917/409073--dc23
LC record available at https://lccn.loc.gov/2016008590

CONTENTS

FOREWORD

Gregory Hood is a brilliant stylist with a great sense of humor as well as a firm grasp of the issues facing white America. I found these essays a pleasure to read, and I was impressed again and again by the depth of his insight into complex issues.

For example, he has a very thorough grasp of the lunacy of mainstream, *National Review*-type conservatism that conceptualizes America as nothing more than a set of abstract ideas centered around keeping the economy functioning—a "conservatism" that proposes that the economy couldn't possibly function without importing tens of millions of skilled and unskilled laborers, with no concern at all for the cohesion of the society, for the inevitable ethnic stratification that it will cause, not to mention the ethnic interests of the traditional American white majority. As he notes in "For Others and Their Posterity" (the title is a wonderful comment on the pathological sense of altruism toward the rest of the world that is now prescribed by our elites), these conservatives think these immigrants "are just like us." They're not.

It's especially encouraging that Mr. Hood came to his views by being repulsed by what he experienced as a college student—the endless victimology being preached by privileged professors who seemed oblivious that they had become pillars of a hierarchical, oppressive, anti-white system, although they rather seem to like the anti-white part. I rather suspect that many other white college students are entertaining similar thoughts, particularly now with the rise of Black Lives Matter and other examples of the triumph of the intolerant Left that are so much a part of college life today. The rise of Donald Trump with his opposition to political correctness and his populist themes emphasizing how American policies on immigration and trade are driven by corrupt special interests is likely having a similar effect in making millions of white people aware of just how corrupt the system is.

Gregory Hood was definitely ahead of the curve in developing his views as a college student, but it's apparent that the rest of America is having a similar awakening. He is already an important voice on the side of white America, and I look forward to reading his future essays as ideas like his become mainstream in America and throughout the West.

Kevin MacDonald

March 2016

KEVIN MACDONALD was, before his retirement, Professor of Psychology at California State University—Long Beach. He is the Editor of *The Occidental Observer* and *The Occidental Quarterly*. He is the author of *A People That Shall Dwell Alone: Judaism as a Group Evolutionary Strategy* (1994), *Separation and Its Discontents: Toward an Evolutionary Theory of Anti-Semitism* (1998), and *The Culture of Critique: An Evolutionary Analysis of Jewish Involvement in Twentieth-Century Intellectual and Political Movements* (1998), as well as *Cultural Insurrections: Essays on Western Civilization, Jewish Influence, and Anti-Semitism* (2007).

PREFACE

Sometimes, you can only judge something properly from a distance. Looking back on the writings contained in this compilation, I realize this is really a book about the collapse of the conservative movement.

The most widely read piece in this book, "A White Nationalist Memo to White Male Republicans," was written in the aftermath of Barack Obama's surprising (to conservatives) re-election. But really, every essay in this book is about how "conservative" institutions, religious groupings, and shibboleths have failed the European Americans who count on them to articulate and defend their interests.

From the perspective of 2016, it's easy to see how some of these writings predicted the rise of the Alt Right and the disruptive effect of Republican presidential candidate Donald Trump, "The Last American," whose importance is addressed in the concluding essay of this volume.

This book is about disillusionment. It's about the loss of faith in both spiritual and political authorities. And it's about being dragged kicking and screaming into accepting a worldview I'd rather avoid. But the truth is the truth. And reality cannot be denied, no matter how badly we wish it would go away.

The Introduction will tell you about how I came to my current views, while the section on "White Nationalism" is a direct attack on many of the egalitarian principles of the American Founding. It may be bracing reading for someone coming from a conservative background.

If you are reading me for the first time, you may want to start with the section on "The Failure of Conservatism," which attempts to explain the conservative movement in the United States. The next section on "Religion and Guns" is a deliberate echo of Barack Obama's notorious comments about Americans "clinging to their guns and religion" because of discomfort with social change. Here, we get into the deeper reasons why many American conservatives and progressives believe what they do, and why a radical rethinking is so necessary.

And finally, there's Trump, whose story, as of this writing, has not yet concluded. One thing we can say for certain is that things will never be the same for the American Right.

I'd like to thank Greg Johnson and Counter Currents Publishing for refusing to let me abandon this project. It would not have been published without his support. I also wish to thank Kevin MacDonald for his Foreword and Jared Taylor, Jack Donovan, F. Roger Devlin, Ramzpaul, and Richard Spencer for their blurbs.

I'd like to dedicate this book not just to those readers who already agree with me but to those who don't. Especially to those who find themselves outraged and even offended by this book and what it represents.

After all, writing political and social commentary is an expression of hope. I don't write for myself or even for those who are already on my side, but for those of my people still lost in this world of lies. If you're not a White Nationalist, don't be afraid to check your premises and question your own beliefs as you read along. You may find you have more in common with me than you think.

If there's one message I want European Americans to take away from this, it's that we are all in this together, collectively, whether we like it or not. We might as well act like it. Even though I rip on the American Founding in this work, I can only think of the quote from Benjamin Franklin in response to King George's III demand for submission—"We must, indeed, all hang together, or most assuredly we shall all hang separately."

In the Alt Right, one of the most popular metaphors is "taking the Red Pill." It's an often painful process to wake up from a pleasant dream. But you can't stay asleep forever. And once you see the world for how it is, there's no going back.

By purchasing this book, you've made a courageous decision. By continuing to read, you're making another. I can't thank you all enough.

Gregory Hood
April 2016

INTRODUCTION
AN AMERICAN SON

> TONY SOPRANO: The morning of the day I got sick, I been thinking. It's good to be in something from the ground floor. I came in too late for that, I know. But lately, I'm getting the feeling that I came in at the end. The best is over.
> DR. MELFI: Many Americans, I think, feel that way.
> TONY: I think about my father. He never reached the heights like me. But in a lotta ways he had it better. He had his people. They had their standards. They had pride. Today, whadda we got?
>
> —*The Sopranos*, Episode 1, "Pilot"

I always felt cheated.

It wasn't because I lacked for anything. I had an idyllic childhood. My childhood was so normal that in the new America, I'm a freak. Two parents (of differing sexes, a necessary clarification these days), a nice house in the suburbs, a stay-at-home mom, a hard-working father with a stable, nonpolitical job. A yard, a friendly dog, home-cooked meals, and a kitchen always bursting with food. A family that would get me through anything—if there were anything to get through.

There's no trauma in my past. No abuse. No bullying at school. No diseases. No racial slurs around the dinner table. No terrible secrets or horrible injuries to overcome. Sensible Center-Left political views. No guns. No violence. Up until the time I stepped into a boxing ring well into adulthood, I had never been in a real fight in my life. After all, what was there to fight about?

Church on Sundays in the denomination of that relaxed American Christianity that holds everyone—Jew or Gentile—is going to heaven, except serial killers or Nazis. And while it was a majority-white neighborhood, it was hardly segregated. Everyone hung out with everyone else. Why wouldn't you?

Yet despite this background, I knew something was deeply wrong with the world I lived in. I eventually found my way into the most hated, marginalized, and repressed social movement in the world. I joined the ranks of a group of people who are universally portrayed by the media as violent, extreme, and crazy. And despite a lifetime of internalizing a certain narrative about history, morality, and politics preached from every organ of culture in the West, I now define myself by its exact opposite.

I am a White Nationalist. I'm writing this to convince you that you should be a White Nationalist too—if you aren't already. And more than that, I'm writing to tell you that there is almost nothing of this country that can be saved—or should be.

The great imperative of our time is for the white European population within the United States to secure its existence by creating a homeland independent of the present American system. All other platforms, programs, and issues are distractions or deceptions. All other political movements, creeds, and beliefs matter only insofar as they lead people towards or away from our position.

I know this to be the truth. I know this mission to be the purpose of my time upon this Earth. I know no cause is more important.

And yet I can't help but wonder: how the hell did I end up here?

WHAT IS MY COUNTRY?

I've always loved my country—or at least the idea of it. But the United States of America isn't mine anymore—and if you're white, no matter how much you love it, work for it, or even bleed for it, it's not yours either. And it's not because of Barack Obama, or Bill Clinton, or even the so-called Civil Rights Movement. It hasn't been ours for a long, long time. Maybe it never really was. Of course, there are plenty of *Born on the Fourth of July*-style coming of age stories where the protagonist rejects his patriotic upbringing to lose himself in a new identity built on "social justice" or *faux* cultural rebellion. This is hardly that. I reject nothing about the way I was raised—a stable family, a reliable income, and loving parents *should be* the norm. Nor do I react with some kind of exaggerated disgust towards the philistine "'Merica" that is so easy to criticize. "There is a great deal of ruin in a nation," and America is no different.

I could say that I'm simply defending the communities like those I came from—and the right of whites to live in them. I could say that—but it isn't really true. The 1950s idealized by the stereotypical American conservative are gone—and they weren't that great to begin with.

Another critic might say that I'm just one of those born revolutionaries who would dissent against any order at all. Today, the entire national and international power structure, political system, and moral code is built around suppressing white identity and European Identitarian politics. So I simply picked the most contrarian thing you could be—the equivalent of a Russian in 1890 deciding that he is a Communist. But that's not it either.

I was never drawn to revolution. My politics don't derive from suburban *ennui*. I was dragged to this position, and I fought it kicking and screaming every step of the way. When all is said and done, I want to win so I don't have to do this anymore. I want a normal job and a normal life in a homeland for my people that won't need professional revolutionaries, dissident writers, or the loathsome profession of "activism."

The truth is something deeper, something that was always there, from the earliest point I can remember. American life can still be prosperous, orderly, and enjoyable, but there's something deeply wrong and sick beneath the surface. It's like a horror movie where the protagonist walks through an idyllic town. Everything seems perfect, but there's something ominous you can't put your finger on. There's a nameless terror behind every smile or friendly wave. And as the film rolls on, it gets harder and harder to pretend it's not there.

There is something deeply wrong with this country. It's easy—even clichéd—to point to the symptoms. The skyrocketing rates of prescription drugs people take just to get through the day, the stabbings and shootings at elementary schools, the collapsing families, the barely veiled hostility between parents and children, the way Americans utterly drop out of their own lives, disappearing into a fantasy world of video games, entertainment, or celebrity junk culture. Despite a surface level of material prosperity undreamed of throughout most of human history, most Americans seem to be driven by a despairing, raging hysteria. They are at war with themselves and with everyone around them.

Just think for a moment how odd it is that we expect children to turn against their families when they become adults. That women idolize careerist celebrities without any clear accomplishments—but don't want children. That men pursue perpetual adolescence. That our media celebrates people who can't decide what sex—or even species—they are. That the smartest people in our society frantically promote an ideology that dredges up the worst within us—weakness, decadence, and an ironic condescension towards past accomplishments. That our entire society seems to be built upon deliberately destroying everything we inherited—and that the loudest voices telling us to pursue equality mysteriously accrue vast personal wealth from these efforts. Was it always like this? Were people always so petty and weak? Were men always judged not by what they did, but whether they were "racist"? What most people praised as the ideal, I found pathetic. And so I felt cheated. I felt something deeply important had been stolen from me—and I didn't have the knowledge to say what it was.

I wasn't a Radical Traditionalist when I was young. I didn't know about the "Kali Yuga" or some grand theory of decline. I wasn't into occult philosophy or alternative history—I was into baseball. I was just a normal American kid who felt that the great battles and heroes were all in the past—and somehow all that was left was this small world of small people.

It started like this, a vague wonder if this was all there is. When on a field trip or a vacation I always felt an odd resentment for the people who climbed on statues or smiled for pictures in front of a memorial. The cold statues seemed more alive than the people. The tourists seemed an insult to a better past filled with better men.

The Bible speaks of a time when the angels of God mixed with the women of Earth, and "there were giants in the earth in those days . . . mighty men which were of old, men of renown." Where were they now? The heroes of the past seemed as foreign as the giants of myth. Far better to disappear into fantasy, leading empires on computer games or reading books about ancient heroes who did something more than complain about racism. Looking around at the white males who disappear into a world of fantasy every chance they get, I knew I wasn't alone.

Even in school, I had the impression that the End of History had arrived, even if I didn't know enough then to call it that. At a certain point, the story of America—and the story of humanity—stopped being about the warriors, the pioneers, and the creators. Instead, it became a story about the victims, the people who built nothing but now had a right to the things other people had made. Our morality demanded it. The nation and the world we lived in had been created, and now all that was left was to point out inequalities and distribute resources accordingly.

And so we were told the great hero wasn't a warrior or a scholar—but a social justice activist. It wasn't the creator or the conqueror—but the weakling who has special rights precisely because of his inferiority.

Nietzsche writes of the Last Man, the man who has discovered happiness, "and blinks." The democratic age ends with "men without chests," leading small lives pursuing petty pleasures, looking down upon the ideas of greatness, struggle, and accomplishment. But this isn't what we have. There are many full of passionate intensity and willingness to sacrifice. But the ideal they sacrifice for is the destruction of ideals, the promotion of "equality," the abolition of "racism" or "hierarchy."

And I found it pathetic.

Like so many others, my awakening to what was at stake came during college. Needless to say, the classes were a joke, and the degree was largely a waste. It was an ideological training camp, albeit one experienced through the haze of all but continuous alcohol and drug intake. Like many liberal arts majors, I found class an afterthought—and even at a supposedly difficult college, it was a simple matter to fit in straight As between bouts of degeneracy.

But academics wasn't the point. That became clear from the moment I set foot on campus. There was nothing, literally nothing, which could not be deconstructed. Toilets were gender exclusive and therefore evil. Statues on campus had to be torn down or buildings renamed. During class, I saw one black student suddenly burst into a fury because someone casually mentioned the cafeteria was serving "brownies."

But I was stuck there. And so I let the school do its work. I opened everything to question. I saw the structural realities of power underneath every dialogue, every class, every student organization. I saw how the personal is political.

But more than that, I saw that they had it precisely backwards. *They* were the system. *They* were the structural inequality. Using what they taught me, I deconstructed the deconstructionists. I saw what a fighting politics could be: Left-wing techniques and social analysis mobilized for Right-wing ends. When a tenured professor whose only credential seems to be her gender or skin color is shrieking at you about "privilege," it becomes abundantly clear that American higher education is just a very expensive exercise in ideological misdirection.

But why I identified with the Right was something deeper, something primal. I had no reactionary illusions about what my country was—*Lies My Teacher Told Me* and *A People's History of the United States* were textbooks, part of the System's curriculum. I didn't come from a Right-wing background. But there was something sickening, something that would physically nauseate me, in the way that the campus Left deliberately promoted ugliness, spat upon everything the country had accomplished, and rejoiced at the destruction of the historic American nation.

The turning point came with one of those racially charged campus controversies that dominate American universities. Older Americans nostalgically donating to their *alma maters* don't really seem to understand just how bad it has gotten. In this particular case, some campus conservatives had fallen afoul of the black students at the school, and seemingly the entire black population of the school came to confront them. After all, they had nothing else to do.

I had no involvement in the activism or the response. I was not politically active during college. I simply sat in the back and listened, unnoticed. The black students alternately raged and cried, threatened violence or lapsed into maudlin self-pity. The handful of white students instantly turned on each other, apologizing and changing their positions. They were terrified—and they were right to be, as they were confronted by a numerically superior and racially motivated mob that had the explicit backing of the school administration.

I walked home from that incident changed. The blunt expression of racial solidarity had shocked me to my core. I began to understand that not everyone is just a white person, some of them with deeper tans. They really aren't like us—and, absent a white majority, the cultural norms and institutions Americans take for granted simply will not exist.

The American Right has always had at its fringe those who connected the dots between the United States and the European-American population that ultimately created and sustains it. Ultimately, as a defensive measure, I awakened to my racial identity. I understood that everything I valued—and everything worth preserving in a declining world—was ultimately dependent on the European-American population.

Conservatives like James Burnham long ago defined the slow retreat of Western civilization, as do mainstream figures like Pat Buchanan and Mark Steyn. I immersed myself in the "counter-jihad" movement. I studied the Minutemen and the responses to mass illegal immigration in the American Southwest. And I placed my faith in the American conservative movement and the traditional tripartite platform of limited government, traditional values, and a strong national defense.

Unfortunately, it didn't take long to see that American conservatism didn't really do much on the issues that matter. On illegal immigration, many Republicans and conservative leaders seemed to actually favor the invasion. A so-called strong national defense was more concerned with defending the borders of countries in the Middle East than our own.

But more than that, I had a slowly dawning awareness that conservatives, at a deep level, did not want to win. They did not want to engage on the issues that mattered. Indeed, they even lacked a real definition of victory. The conservative movement was, as Joe Sobran said, "a game, a way of making a living."

Millions of American conservatives have come to this realization and organized to defend conservatism from itself in the form of various patriot groups or the Tea Party movement. But I started to come to a different conclusion. I slowly began to understand that conservatism—and America—could not be saved from itself.

Even more than that, I began to appreciate, if only distantly, the contempt artists and intellectuals have for what is called bourgeois civilization. I think your average white American, just like your average American conservative, has decent values. But every instinct they have is defensive and conflict-averse. They will sacrifice anything and surrender everything in order to have another moment of peace. They will march voluntarily into the camps—indeed, they seem indifferent that what was once their country has become an especially large combination of a gulag and an insane asylum.

Julius Evola wrote in *Men Among the Ruins*:

> We must concede that, *per se*, an anti-bourgeois stance has a reason for existence. I do not mean bourgeois so much in the sense of an economic class, but rather its counterpart: there is an intel-

lectual world, an art, custom, and general view of life that, having been shaped in the last century parallel to the revolution of the Third Estate, appear as empty, decadent, and corrupt. A resolute overcoming of all this is one of the conditions required to solve the present crisis of our civilization.[1]

An American *qua* American is incapable of this. Even though mass immigration and outsourcing have ensured that the American middle class is in desperate retreat, Americans still define themselves as a middle-class country. More importantly, the American Right explicitly defines its purpose as the defense of bourgeois classical liberalism—the defense of "life, liberty, and property," to use George Mason's phrase. Even as the substance and population of the country changes, we continue to cling to abstractions like "the Constitution."

What I was confronting was the problem of every modern conservative: how do you save institutions that are already corrupted? And eventually, I came to understand the truth: *you don't.*

WHY I GAVE UP ON THE AMERICAN STATE—& REDISCOVERED MY PEOPLE

It's no small thing to give up on your country. It is part of you, as much a part of you as your hometown or the faith of your youth. But people move away from those things too.

I never lost faith in what this country accomplished. It is easy for the European New Right to sneer at America—the land that progressed straight to decadence, without

---

[1] Julius Evola, *Men Among the Ruins: Post-War Reflections of a Radical Traditionalist*, trans. Guido Stucco, ed. Michael Moynihan (Rochester, Vermont: Inner Traditions, 2002), p. 271.

an interval of civilization. But the fact remains that this country—and no other—landed on the moon. We conquered an entire continent through war and struggle, perhaps the greatest military achievement of the entire millennium. We built the industries that created the modern world—and continue to create the technology that will be used in the world to come. America is the greatest military power in the world, the greatest economic power in the world, and the greatest cultural influence in the world. And, most important of all, until very recently, Americans defined themselves as whites and their country as a white nation.

And there are elements of that historic American nation that will always resonate with European Americans. The conquest of the West. The last stand at the Alamo. The Marines storming Iwo Jima. Bunker Hill, Pickett's Charge, the Lewis and Clark expedition, the building of the Transcontinental Railroad—who dares say that America lacks the legends, history, and heroes of Europe? This land of ours was sanctified with the blood of European warriors since the coming of the Pilgrim Fathers.

Yet America's fall was inevitable. If the past century has taught us anything, it is that ideas are eventually taken to their logical conclusion. And whatever the triumphs the European people have achieved on this continent, they were ultimately in the service of a Founding Creed boiled down to "All men are created equal."

It doesn't matter that Thomas Jefferson didn't mean this in the literal sense. Nor is it a contradiction that America, for most of its history, has thought of herself as a white nation. America at its core can only be defined as one of two ways—as an extension of Europe on the continent of North America, or as a deliberate separation from the Old World. And while there is much to admire in the American Revolution and in the great achievements of the United States, at its core the American ideal is that "we have it in our power to begin the world anew." And so we did—and destroyed ourselves.

"America" did not accomplish anything. Whites did. European-Americans did. "American" accomplishments overwhelmingly belong to them—and them alone. But the white historic American nation and "America" are two different things. The latter is an ideological construct at its core, defined by natural rights, universal egalitarianism, and material aspirations.

Looking around the contemporary United States, who can doubt that America is simply evolving into the logical conclusion of its founding ideals? Like the Comedian in *Watchmen*, who is asked "What happened to the American Dream?," we have to answer, "It came true. You're looking at it."

To be a European American with a future means to confront the lie that is the American ideal. All men are *not* created equal. Rights are a product of power, not the gift of a Deist "God" whose will is reinterpreted every other week. The upward development of the race is the purpose of the state, not accumulating money by systematically degrading it. And we have more in common with our racial kinsmen in England, Germany, the Netherlands, and the other nations of the Occident than with our non-white "fellow Americans." Our Republic is no longer a melting pot, but a trash can. America today is simply enforced mediocrity.

Another world is possible—but there is something standing in the way. That something is America. Her existence drafts the past accomplishments of European Americans in service of policies and powers that are destroying them. The "mystic chords of memory," as Lincoln called them, are less a source of solidarity and sacrifice than a tool of emotional blackmail against whites who know that something is deeply wrong but are afraid to break with a sanctified past.

Waking up from the American Dream means recognizing that American ideals have been tried, tested, and found wanting. They have led us to a country where all that is best is systematically sacrificed in the service of what is worst. Americans sense it—but resist what is to be done. To continue to believe in the Dream is to remain in a troubled sleep.

But we are awake. We are not "Americans," for how can one be a citizen of an abstraction? We are Europeans, whites who have conquered the North American wilderness and are prepared to claim our birthright of a nation where we are free to be ourselves. We know that this farce you call a country is a nightmare that just rolls on and on, and we want no part of it.

We are not willing to die to make the world safe for garbage food, garbage culture, and garbage people, but we are willing to work and if need be fight for an organic society worthy of service and sacrifice. We want to offer what is best in the service of something even greater. We want a homeland—and we mean to have it.

That which was best about America is still ours. But we don't need this failed experiment anymore. We can be something better. But that can't happen if we just go back to sleep and pretend that when we wake up in the morning everything will be ok.

It gives me no joy to write this. It will be difficult, and in the short term, it's always easier to remain asleep. But as I look back over my own life's journey, I realize that politics and history are not so much about society, but about ourselves. What kind of people are we?

Patrick Henry once asked, "Is life so dear, or peace so sweet, as to be purchased at the price of chains and slavery?" Are we willing to accept the living degradation that American life has become? And if we are, what does that say about us?

I've heard authors and politicians define the core of America as "optimism." But as Spengler said, "Optimism is cowardice." We need the courage to break with pleasant illusions. Our nation is of blood, not of paper. We need to wake up to our own dispossession, and the forces that made it possible. And we need to create a homeland in order to take back our own souls from a culture that has become a poison. To do less is to betray that which is best within us, we who created and can surpass that beautiful lie we called the United States of America.

Counter-Currents/*North American New Right*,
December 31, 2015

WAKING UP FROM THE
AMERICAN DREAM

THE AMERICAN DREAM VS. THE AMERICAN NATION

The *dénouement* came with the election of Barack Hussein Obama. It changed nothing in the structure of real power. The same people controlled the American regime both before and after Election Day 2008. But the symbolic importance of a black man being inaugurated as head of state in a capital city named after a white slaveholder had a power all its own. Blacks in America shrieked on social networking sites that they "owned" America. Liberal whites cried in delight and basked in their own self-satisfaction. And conservative whites finally had that vague sense of occupation that liberals felt when the White House was controlled by the likes of Nixon, Reagan, or George W. Bush.

Of course, it was business as usual in the national security deep state, the financial system, and the media. But under the Obama Administration, the civic creed of multiculturalism, anti-racism, and diversity took on an increasingly frantic, even unhinged tone. Every mild racial insult, expression of political incorrectness, or "coming out" of a worthless celebrity was cause for hysterical condemnation or celebration.

There was a hint of North Koreans' forced grieving for Kim Jong Il in Americans' reaction to the death of Nelson Mandela. Terms like "cisgender" and "white privilege" became part of the conversations of ostensibly normal people. American society increasingly resisted satire, as college students were animated—even outraged—by the existence of separate toilets for men and women. And within the media, opposition to gay marriage was treated as all but equivalent to support for racial segregation.

There are no limits to this process. Nor should Americans be surprised. The tragedy of America is that ideas are eventually taken to their logical conclusions.

THE AMERICAN DREAM

The American nation is being killed by the American Dream. As George Carlin once said: "They call it the American Dream because you have to be asleep to believe it." Of course, this was at the end of a long rant about how "the owners" of the country, by which he meant the rich white males who tell us all to believe in God and want obedient workers, actually propagate this idea to defend their economic interests. The mostly liberal crowd therefore felt free to applaud.

As the saying goes, "If I tell you that there are powerful people who are oppressing you to defend their own interests, you'll call me a progressive, a liberal, and a reformer. If I tell you who those people are, you'll call me a Nazi."

The American Dream defines what we are as a country. The concept has many meanings, but at its core, it's the idea that this country gives a person, regardless of his background, the opportunity to break whatever bonds are holding him back, be it poverty, stultifying tradition, or government repression. In so doing, he can build the life of his dreams—the unhindered "pursuit of happiness." Often, this centers on material progress—sometimes, something so literal as saying, "the American Dream is home ownership in the suburbs." After all, in George Mason's less poetic formulation, classical liberalism is about "life, liberty, and property."

The Beltway Right insists that this Dream still exists for everyone. In this telling, on some glorious day we will all become job creators and small business owners. To use a slogan the Republicans deployed during the 2012 Presidential elections, "we built that" independent of society. To question this is to attack the core idea of the country, to be un-American. Indeed, one of the most common attacks of Republican presidential candidates against President Obama is the idea that he doesn't believe enough in American Exceptionalism, the idea that America is unique, somehow more unique than every other country in the world.

The Left, of course, says that the Dream isn't fair enough, since class divisions and racial differences exist. There is patriarchy, white privilege, heteronormativity, cisgenders, and all the rest that are eternally "holding us back." And new enemies of the people are always being created.

However, the core idea for the two groups is still the same: self-creation and the acquisition of wealth by everyone is the definition of the good. The Beltway American Right holds to the faith that this essential equality and economic opportunity exists and will always exist, all evidence to the contrary.

Meanwhile, the Left seizes the reformist mantle. They can never be satisfied because there will always be inequality, which the American Right concedes is bad. Thus, the Left has an eternal claim on the moral high ground.

Both sides agree with the profoundly anti-Traditionalist idea that America is nothing but a place to make money.

Yet despite this core ideological agreement, the political debate in America is driven by something primal under the surface. The Left insists that there must be government men with guns to ensure that "everyone" (especially non-whites) gets an equal shot. At the same time, the Left permanently defines the existing capitalist system as a racist, patriarchal system that is run by white men. The Left simultaneously has a monopoly on an ideological defense of the current system and the language of revolution.

Or, in the words of Rage Against the Machine, "For it's

the end of history. It's caged and frozen still. There is no other pill to take, so swallow the one that made you ill." In this view, radical, individualist capitalism is unjust precisely because it is rooted in racism—economic differences are simply a consequence of racial injustice. The band goes on to rant about the *Niña, Pinta,* and *Santa María,* and the noose and overseer and the never-ending exploitation of the noble colored masses by the White Man. This is essentially the pattern of all contemporary American progressive activism. Justice will arrive when the white man hands back his ill-gotten gains.

In response, simple reactionaries that they are, the Beltway Right defends the system against these attacks. To some extent, they accept the Leftist critique that the existing capitalist system is the property of whites—they simply deny that this is unfair and claim that everyone, of every race, can gain admission to the American Dream and the goodies it contains. They even do this as the economic elite of the country grows explicitly anti-white, both funding and executing anti-white affirmative action policies, agitating for unlimited Third World immigration, and eagerly promoting an ever-more destructive cultural agenda. The conservative response is generally to call for more tax cuts. It is an opposition doomed to fail—perhaps even designed to fail.

But even though this political struggle is nothing but shadow-boxing, the rhetoric and emotions raised seem to grow more savage each election cycle. This is because there remains a residual American patriotism recognized by both sides in the culture war. The Beltway Right has claimed it; the American Left is suspicious of it. Even though the Beltway Right defends America largely on economic grounds, the emotional motivation underlying it is rooted in deeper cultural and implicitly racial beliefs about what constitutes the authentic American identity. The flag, the military, and certain motifs of what Peter

Brimelow calls the "historic American nation" still resonate as either a positive example or something to be
feared.
The conquest of the West. The Marine Corps. The
Founding Fathers. All of these are mythologized by conservatives and demonized by liberals. And if anything, this
kind of implicitly white patriotism is increasing among
European Americans.
Glenn Beck has built a hugely profitable internet and
radio media empire that positively fetishizes the Founding
Fathers. The American Revolution is undergoing a dramatic spike in interest in the publishing industry. A huge,
implicitly white political movement borrows the symbolism of the Boston Tea Party.
And yet while all this is going on, no one on the mainstream Right would ever recognize—let alone defend—a
distinct European-American identity and collective interest. At the same time, even as the Left is ever-more eager
to call the American Right "racist," its policy prescriptions
are still grounded in the traditional American rhetoric of
"freedom" and "equality."
Both sides are discussing trivia about the tax code,
debt, and health care; both sides are motivated by primal
racial and cultural motivations that neither dares recognize; and yet both are arguing within a broadly shared
context of values of "freedom," "equality," and material
prosperity.

THE CULTURE, THE CREED, & THE DREAM
One of the more tragic figures of the recent past was
Samuel Huntington, perhaps the most significant political
scientist this country produced in the last century. Anyone who has gone to graduate school will study his books
in several courses simultaneously, on subjects as diverse as
democratization in Latin America to civil-military rela-
tions.

And yet, he'll be remembered in the media, insofar as he will be remembered at all, for his analysis of the so-called Clash of Civilizations, a challenge to the End of History.[1] He'll also be outright demonized for his final book, *Who Are We? The Challenges to America's National Identity*, which attempted to answer the elusive question of what constitutes the American identity.[2]

Huntington identified an American Creed as central to what defined the country. However, the American culture was also present, and while it contributed to the development of the Creed, it was distinct from it. The American Creed of limited government, suspicion of royal authority, and all the rest of the classical liberal boilerplate we are used to was identified with the dissenting Protestantism brought to the United States by English settlers. However, Huntington stated that while the American Creed and the American identity is elastic, it is not infinitely so: "America cannot become the world and still be America."

The book was reviewed in a few places, but it made no real impact on the culture. The only politician of any note who actually talked about it was Tom Tancredo. He named his radio show after it and gave a few speeches about it, of course peppered with the usual denials that this had anything to do with race. The Southern Poverty Law Center responded by calling his speeches White Nationalist screeds which claimed only White Anglo-Saxon Protestant culture was American.

On the Left there was outright hatred. When Huntington—the most distinguished scholar of his generation, a dean of Harvard's Kennedy School of Government, and a New Deal liberal—came to speak at a school in Texas, he

---

[1] Samuel Huntington, *The Clash of Civilizations and the Remaking of World Order* (New York: Simon and Schuster, 1996)

[2] Samuel Huntington, *Who Are We? The Challenges to America's National Identity* (New York: Simon and Schuster, 2005).

was protested by Hispanics calling him a racist and a Nazi. He died not long afterward. This should serve as a warning about relying on "credentials" to generate a rational response.

What may be surprising to some is that the American Right called Huntington un-American—because he was not optimistic enough. The Claremont Institute declared he didn't show enough respect for "that optimism [which] sets us apart from much of the world, fuels our entrepreneurial spirit, encourages immigrants seeking a better life, and inspires us to encourage democracy around the globe."[3] It called for faith.

Both the American Right and the American Left believe in the American Creed, at least rhetorically. But both also dismiss that there actually is anything that can be called a distinct American culture. Indeed, even while the American Right relies on the defense of American culture to give it its emotional impetus, it either cannot define it or refuses to acknowledge that it could possibly exclude anyone else on earth. If this seems odd, simply recall how the overwhelmingly white American conservative movement furiously attacks anyone who dares broach the subject of white identity—and furthermore, habitually attacks the Left as being white supremacist and racist.

Instead of the Culture, we have the American Creed. And once the Creed becomes a civic religion, we have the American Dream—the prosperity gospel of a nation. The American Dream of material prosperity is linked to the ideas of constitutionalism, limited government, freedom, and "liberty." This Dream is so powerful that the strongest right-leaning critique of the existing system comes from the libertarians, who believe that the United States of America doesn't talk *enough* about material prosperity

---

[3] http://www.claremont.org/crb/article/culture-versus-creed/

and limited government.

A popular internet film from libertarians is actually entitled *The American Dream*.[4] It centers on the Rothschilds, the Federal Reserve, the inflation tax, and other themes familiar to the libertarian Right, especially those that flirt with critiques of Jewish power. It's well-made, funny, and its multiple postings combined boast well over three million views. But of course, the premise is that a stupid, ignorant, weak, blue-eyed white guy must be educated and informed by a charismatic and masculine black guy.

Libertarians, the rising force in the American Right, are in some ways even worse than the Beltway Right that exists today. While mainstream conservatism and even neoconservatism depends on a kind of perverted reading of American nationhood, libertarianism denies it altogether. The genocide of the Indians, slavery, the racist Drug War, and Southern segregation are all part of the tapestry of evil woven by statism. Whereas much of American libertarianism may have been grounded in implicit whiteness, and the movement is still implicitly white, it is gradually growing more explicitly anti-white than even the kind of conservatism advocated by *The Weekly Standard*.

Thus, throughout the entire spectrum of American political thought, there is fundamental agreement about the desirability of the American Dream of material prosperity and classical liberalism. To be sure, Left and Right have two slightly different ways of looking at it.

The Left sneers at it as hypocrisy, but doesn't ultimately question the endgame. Ultimately, America is about making sure that everyone gets to be equally prosperous and define his own existence from the comfort of his Tumblr account. The more moderate Left might say that America's glory is that it pronounced a creed of equality for all. We always make progress (as we take power away

---

[4] https://www.youtube.com/watch?v=ZPWH5TlbloU

from the hated white males is left unsaid), but "there is always more to be done." America is defined by the progression towards equality.

The Right responds with an ever-more frantic attachment to the idea of freedom, liberty, and limited government, coupled with an insistence on equality of opportunity rather than equality of outcome. The conservatives will say America already is free. The libertarians will say it should be free, but is bound by statism. But both will say the ideal is a proposition nation where every individual can try to create as much prosperity as possible. America is defined by the progression towards ever-greater economic growth.

These ideas are symbiotic and complementary. Both the American Left and Right contribute arguments towards breaking apart the historic American nation, either as an obstacle to equality or an obstacle to growth. Both urge the replacement of the actually existing nation and culture in pursuit of an abstract ideal. And both, ultimately, define the ideal in terms of liberation from the old— either from regressive social norms or state limitations on economic activity. America may have been, in the words of Robert Kagan, one of its neoconservative defenders, "born to die."[5]

In its own way, the American Dream is the most aggressively egalitarian concept in history, far more devastating in its effects than any doctrine dreamed of by Marx or Lenin. It utterly liquidates any consideration of community ties, religious obligations, or traditional ideals in favor of an unrestrained individualism grounded in absolute equality. This ideological egalitarianism, paradoxically, enables increasing economic inequality and the entrenchment of the financial system. We are told we are all

---

[5] http://www.examiner.com/article/born-to-die-examining-the-united-states-on-the-fourth-of-july

created equal—which leads to the unrestrained reign of wealth, unhindered by community responsibility, ethnic solidarity, or even *noblesse oblige.*

The doctrine of equality of race, gender, culture, and human quality enables the permanent entrenchment of a power structure elite that denies its own elitism. We have a ruling class that is secure precisely because it denies any hierarchical basis to its lordship. Its power is unchallenged because it denies it has power. It rules because it flatters its serfs that they rule themselves—in fact, telling them that no one rules them at all. And, unlike the high cultures of the past, the cultural products produced by our elite are far more degenerate, disgusting, and ugly than anything that exists among working communities.

Thus, America's transformation into a culture that would have disgusted the patriots of the past is not a departure from the American ideal. In many ways, it is a fulfillment of that ideal. While the pendulum of political power may occasionally swing back and forth from the Republicans to the Democrats, the core ideal of wealth acquisition through the unlimited expansion of freedom and the abolition of privilege is never challenged at a fundamental level.

WAS AMERICA'S DECLINE INEVITABLE?

The present climate is the culmination of centuries of egalitarian momentum. This is not a particularly unique observation. With the rise of the Dark Enlightenment, the American Revolution has come under critical purview from an authentic North American New Right. Many intellectuals conclude that the American experiment was destined to be a failure, grounded as it was in egalitarian Enlightenment nonsense. Therefore, we should raise our glasses and give a hearty toast to His Britannic Majesty.

The historical truth is more complicated, as always. One of the driving forces of the Revolution in Virginia was the efforts of Lord Dunmore, the royal governor, to arm black slaves and white indentured servants against property-owning white settlers.

In New England, theological motivations were at the forefront. Insofar as one person can be seen as being primarily responsible for launching the Revolution, it was Sam Adams. Sam Adams is sometimes called the last Puritan because he was a Congregationalist true believer who thought he was doing the Lord's will—and opposed British efforts because he thought they were trying to impose Anglicanism and eventually Catholicism on New England. He said he dreamed of Boston as a "Christian Sparta." It is hard to think of an ideal more foreign to the contemporary United States than a "Christian Sparta" that banned plays and frivolous pursuits.

The Father of our Country, George Washington, was not primarily motivated by egalitarian rhetoric. He was infuriated by British attempts to restrict westward expansion and thought the British were holding the Americans back. His vision of the new nation was that of a "rising empire."

Even Jefferson, the man who wrote that "all men are created equal," went on to condemn in that same document the "merciless Indian savages." Also, although Jefferson was certain that black slavery would someday be brought to an end, he was "equally certain" that blacks and whites could not live together under the same government.

A compelling case can be made that the American Revolutionaries were more racially patriotic than the British Empire, especially in regards to Indian policy. But in the end, that doesn't matter. In the long run, people ultimately believe their own propaganda.

When Sam Adams died, one of the people paying tribute to him was a Catholic bishop—this for a man who opposed Anglicanism because he thought it was a way to smuggle in popery. Today, Boston is the stereotypical center of New England secular liberalism.

George Washington no longer has a holiday in the country he bequeathed—that honor is reserved for Martin Luther King, Jr. The Father of His Country is remembered as a slave-owner, if at all, by non-European Americans.

Jefferson is hoist by his own petard because "all men are created equal" and is today condemned as both a slave-owner and a rapist of black women.

In fact, all of American history before 1965 is largely dismissed as white supremacy. Andrew Sullivan, who occasionally calls himself a conservative, moans that early America was a "genocidal gulag for African-Americans" and questions how he can have a partnership with "proud, defiant and violent slave-holders."[6] However, he gloats, America will transform itself because "whites will be a minority in this country" and thus, presumably, the historic American nation will be eradicated in favor of the American egalitarian ideal. America will be saved, because the historic American people will be replaced.

What authentic American patriots remain respond to the attack on their history largely through protective ignorance or deliberate distortion. One young man I knew who spoke at Tea Party rallies would recite the Declaration of Independence from memory in colonial garb—with the part about the merciless Indian savages omitted. He justified it on the grounds that if Jefferson could see America today, it's what he would have wanted. The American past is justified on the grounds that it *led to* multiculturalism and diversity—even if the heroes of the American past specifically condemned it, or even if today some conservatives think the multicultural rhetoric "goes too far."

---

[6] http://dish.andrewsullivan.com/2014/03/28/a-nation-defined-by-white-supremacy/

The specific grievances and actual motivations of America's great patriots and heroes are eventually overwhelmed by their own simplistic slogans. The relationship is especially complicated because ideas are driven by identity. Kevin Phillips, in his studies of the various civil wars within the Anglosphere, from the English Civil War to the American, says that ethnicity and religion were the biggest determinants of which side you were on. Material interests are important but secondary. But in the end, ideas take on a terrible importance of their own.

Kevin MacDonald has written of how whites, even independent of Jewish power, would occasionally sabotage their own material interests in the service of an ideology, especially because of religious motivations.[7] In the long run, identity can even be formed on ideological lines, as with religious sects who consider racially alien co-religionists to be their "brethren" but ignore their racial or ethnic kinsmen. The civic religion of Americanism is an attempt to do just that—and it just so happens that most of the true believers are white. The patriotic dedication of American whites to the nation of the past has led to an ideological devotion to the anti-white, egalitarian United States of the present.

It doesn't start this way. Material interests, identity, and ideology are tied together, but ultimately, ideology is what endures and is carried along by the terrible process of history. Great men can set in motion things they never could have anticipated. I have no doubt Jefferson, Adams, or even Lincoln would slit their wrists if they saw what they unleashed—but that doesn't mean it wasn't inevitable.

A few examples. Years ago, I saw a libertarian Beltway

---

[7] Kevin MacDonald, "American Transcendentalism: An Indigenous Culture of Critique," *The Occidental Quarterly*, vol. 8, no. 2 (Summer 2008).

operative tell a crowd of social conservatives he could convince them all to support gay marriage. He did, by simply telling them that America is about equality and individual liberty. The conservatives, lacking the vocabulary to challenge the desirability of equality and liberty, felt compelled to go along with this—lest they be un-American.

The point here is not to argue for or against gay marriage—the point is that this technique can be used on literally *every* egalitarian innovation to come, without exception. Give it a decade, and we'll be hearing how Jefferson and Lincoln would have wanted to eliminate gender-segregated toilets. Conservatives will mock it at first, then remain quiet, then surrender to it, and finally take credit for it, having never actually articulated a reason why this is wrong. After all, to question egalitarianism—no matter how extreme—is to question the American Creed and the American Dream of self-creation.

A similar process takes place when libertarians talk about immigration, even when they know mass immigration will destroy all the things they claim to believe in. Many Beltway libertarians know and understand that a Third World America will be a demonstrably less free America. However, they must remain true to their political faith and support open borders, even when it will destroy what they believe in. Other libertarians support open borders precisely *because* it will destroy the historic American nation, which they see as repressive and hypocritical, especially on sexual matters. What replaces it is less important than taking vengeance on the "Red State Fascists" of the present who have violated their own ideals of "liberty."

This is now happening to the country at large. Rather than being a source of strength, the American Creed tells people what they are not allowed to say or do. American whites know something is wrong. They sense vaguely they are being dispossessed. Yet they simultaneously believe they are not allowed to do anything about it without somehow being anti-American.

The American Dream is being taken to its logical conclusion. And the result will be the end of America. To this we say—So Be It.

FREEDOM VS. IDENTITY

Turn on the television. Read a mainstream media website. Try and listen to a politician give a speech. This accumulated filth, this celebration of mediocrity, this Third World carnival of grotesqueries *is* America. When the highest ideals of a nation are freedom, equality, and liberty, how could it lead to anything but this? And to paraphrase Göring, when one hears the word "liberty" today, how can a decent man do anything but draw his revolver?

In marketing, they talk about "the elevator speech," where you have to give your case in the span of an elevator journey, maybe 10 seconds. This is too long. What is our counter to the word "freedom"? What is our counter to the word "equality"? While ideologically, words like *hierarchy* or *greatness* are closer to the essence of the North American New Right, the word *identity* is the most relevant. That's what we're about, and that communicates everything else that needs to be said.

Looking at the American Revolution, we can see how specific grievances and motivations can eventually be turned into historical forces that lead not just to unexpected, but opposite conclusions of what the original activists would want. Therefore, every popular, specific grievance has to be expressed in identitarian terms. Obamacare is a wealth transfer from one racial group to another. The knockout game allows blacks to target whites for beatings with impunity. All this kind of stuff is popular on conservative websites, but always portrayed as a rejection of Martin Luther King's color-blind ideal. Instead, it should be expressed in terms of one group attacking another group.

For example, the League of the South demonstrating against what they call demographic displacement. "They are trying to replace us." This is the best way to communicate the message.

But breaking that loyalty to the larger American ideal—waking up from the American Dream—is still the biggest obstacle. This is hardly an unusual problem. One of the early influences on German National Socialism was the situation of the Germans under the Austro-Hungarian Empire. They were the core of the state; they created the state and sustained it; but the state discriminated against them. The empire's priority was to hold itself together, to appease all the various squabbling ethnicities. The ruling Hapsburgs took the Germans for granted.

One can see the same kind of situation with Russia today, where the somewhat conservative Putin sees his job as holding together Russia's various groups, not advancing the interests of the white Russian people.

Or, to use a fictional example, consider a popular video game from a couple years ago, Skyrim. The player undertakes his quest against the background of a civil war in a cosmopolitan empire composed of several races. The northern province, Skyrim, is the home of the Nords, a blonde-haired people who despise magic, favor two-handed weapons, enjoy the cold, and believe the valorous dead go to a glorious afterlife where they can feast and fight for eternity. (Sounds familiar.)

They created the empire. One of their greatest heroes was actually the first emperor, whom they later deified. They are the backbone of the army and the civil service. However, out of weakness, the empire is forced to sign a treaty with a foreign race—here, elves, who force them to stop worshipping a Nord as a god. The elves believe they are uniquely chosen to lead the other groups—and to enforce this, they have a network of enforcers, spies, and watchdogs—which, though not part of the government, supervise it and make sure the Nords don't get any ideas. (Who does that sound like?)

The player has to choose which side to support—on the one hand, a united empire is in some ways stronger, and it belongs to the Nords in some essential way. On the other hand, the state is mobilized against the Nordic people. Of course, the downside from the modern perspective is that the Nordic freedom fighters are accused of being racists.

Perhaps the closest parallel to the American situation is the timely example of South Africa. The pre-eminent ethnonationalist movement in South Africa was the Afrikaner Resistance Movement (the AWB—Afrikaner Weerstandsbeweging), the Boer nationalist organization headed by the late Eugène Terre'Blanche.

There is a grim joke about white South Africans—they would rather be murdered in their bed than have to make it. But this is not true about Boer nationalists—they knew exactly what their problems were. They knew cheap labor drove their dispossession. They knew international capital was their main enemy. They knew big businesses were meeting with the ANC. They knew traditional Afrikaner institutions had been corrupted. Yet despite their core ideological soundness, the AWB failed miserably to secure the freedom of their people.

The AWB had some personal problems, most notably over an alleged affair between Terre'Blanche and a female reporter. But part of the problem was that they couldn't decide if they were supporting South Africa or breaking away from it. One day there was a call for a Boer homeland. The next day they supported the South African police. They claimed they opposed both communism and capitalism—which of course allowed businessmen to be trotted out, condemning the AWB as socialist. They also used symbols which resembled those of National Social-ism—allowing the liberal church members to condemn them as anti-Christian.

Ultimately, the AWB pushed for a secession plan to se-cure the *Volkstaat*—but were betrayed by conservatives who thought they could get a promise of consideration from Nelson Mandela. Obviously, it didn't work. The AWB petered out in a bombing campaign.

This brings us back to where we are now. We have the challenge of breaking away the core population from the state they created. We have to break the loyalty of a peo-ple towards something they say is theirs, including the personal ambitions tied up in it—careers, ties to institu-tions, and established connections.

Eventually, the smarter people among our population need to reject the larger American empire because they see no way they can rise to the top in it. Part of that may already be happening—after all, even the presidency is now an affirmative action job. But most people still think they can succeed in the existing system if they just keep their heads down—or sell out in a vocal enough manner.

Finally, and most importantly, we have to break our people away from the American Creed. We have to tell them they don't have to believe in the classical liberal ide-as they have been told their entire lives. We have to tell them that equality is the path to a meaningless life.

We have to wake them up from the American Dream.

THE REPUBLIC VS. THE FATHERLAND

The French author Jean Raspail noted that his French Fatherland was betrayed by those who confused Republi-can values with the nation itself.[8] In America, the process is far worse, because the nation was a flawed ideological

---

[8] http://www.occidentaldissent.com/2010/06/23/sam-francis-jean-raspail-and-western-unity/

experiment from the beginning. Yet there is still that "historic American nation" and the institutions and cultural norms associated with it. For European Americans, the flag, the Founding Fathers, the West, and all the rest of it will always mean *something* to us, even as we understand this country was doomed from the beginning. More importantly, they will always mean something to the great majority of European-Americans.

What remains is to mobilize the Fatherland against the Republic—the specific cultural norms and symbols of the historic American nation against the egalitarian values of the founding. Here, there is much to celebrate, and our enemies have done much of the work for us.

For example, in 1775, when revolutionary fervor was actually greater than in much of 1776, members of the Virginia House of Burgesses attended the legislative session dressed like militia members, carrying knives and tomahawks. Sam Adams' scorn towards the effeminate foppery of the European courts is also a model to follow. The ideal of the white man at arms, organized in his own defense, and not at the beck and call of the state, is a recurring motif in the American past and a pillar of early republican (small "r") ideology in the United States. It can also never be tolerated by anti-white forces within the country— even college mascots named "Pioneers" are having to be renamed.

There are symbols and slogans of the American past that can be co-opted and utilized. Everything from the Continental Army to the Alamo is fundamentally the property of the historic European-American nation. After all, what better phrase can be used to justify White Nationalism than "for ourselves and our posterity"?

At the same time, these symbols have to be utilized in the service of an explicitly identitarian and anti-liberal cause. That which is not explicitly for our people inevitably turns against our people with time. The Ron Paul movement so enthusiastically supported by white patriots in 2008 has devolved into an explicitly anti-white libertarian movement that champions open borders, white dispossession, and endlessly harping on the need to reach out to "minorities." White Nationalists can no longer afford such mistakes.

The historic American nation must be separated from the regime. As part of this, minorities should be accurately described as what they are—obedient clients designed to solidify the regime. The current American government sees European Americans as its biggest threat. Nonwhites, utterly dependent by design on government handouts, jobs, and patronage, are the main pillar of support for the existing federal government. If the federal government disappeared tomorrow, whites in North America would thrive. Non-whites would instantly have no place.

For that reason, the primary strategic challenge for white revolutionaries is breaking European Americans' emotional attachment to the state. Each action by the government against the memory of the historic American nation is a propaganda victory in this regard. The refusal of the federal government to fulfill even its most basic responsibilities even while it launches foreign interventions all around the world helps make that case. The European Americans who built, sustain, and fight for the country are treated with contempt, even as illegal immigrants who openly despise the United States constitute a new privileged class. It is precisely those who contribute the least to the country who are most actively rewarded. Therefore, why sacrifice for those who hate you?

While traditional American symbols can be used, traditional American rhetoric cannot. European Americans are not fighting for equality and certainly not for democracy. Liberalism, classical or otherwise, is the problem. European Americans need to fight for identity. They need to fight for a homeland. They need to fight for their very existence and survival. They must fight for the upward development of the race, and of humanity, for the defiant faith that there is something better than the filth we are offered as "freedom." The American Dream has to be replaced with something better—in the words of Harold Covington, it is time to replace the American Dream with the Iron Dream.

AN ANCIENT PEOPLE, A NEW IDEAL

We hold these truths to be self-evident: that all men are created unequal, that a natural aristocracy has been endowed among them by their Creator, and that the purpose of human existence is the upward development of the individual, the ethnic community, and the race. That to secure this development, the state is implemented among men, deriving its authority from those who are willing to establish and defend it, and fight on its behalf.

Not quite the spirit of 1776. But there is still something in the great stories of the American Revolution and in the American past that speaks to the European soul. Our triumphs as a nation came despite, not because of, the flawed ideals of our founding. America accomplished many great things in its history. But those deeds were the product of our people, not hoary slogans that were nothing better than the champagne socialism of their day. There is more value in the deeds themselves, than in the shallow slogans used to justify our rebellion. We are the sons of the North, the race of Europa, the People of the Sun. America is but one of our creations—and the power that created its greatest triumphs is in our blood, not in words on a piece of parchment.

The American Dream can be pleasant on occasion, like a drunken revelry, or a drug-induced haze. But it ends in the dungheap that piles up all around us, and it must be said plainly—this ideology, this culture, this government, and this America is not worth dying for, working for, or even living in. Like an addict, we must awake from the American Dream, or die in our beds, surrounded by filth.

Let our next rebellion be more honest, free of illusion and classical liberal propaganda that's been outdated for centuries. On this continent, let's build the purest expression of our Northern soul, the most glorious triumph of our European spirit. For this is the challenge the present offers—a new dream, a "rising empire," to use Washington's phrase, dedicated to the best within us. And this time, we will rise not in defense of a meaningless "freedom," but in defense of our blood, and in defense of the idea of rising itself, transcending the egalitarian swamp.

It's hard to wake from a pleasant dream. After all, during a dream we can experience the impossible, obtain pleasures without effort, and even when half-awake, retreat back into the soft comfort of our beds.

But we have to awake. Reveille has sounded. The next few decades will determine whether Western Man has a future on the continent his ancestors discovered, explored, settled, built, and fought and died for. The American Dream is over—and it has to be replaced with the waking vision of the White Republic.

Counter-Currents/North American New Right,
March 31 and April 1–4, 2014

FOR OTHERS & THEIR PROSPERITY

There exists no simpler, shorter, or more poetic expression of nationalism than five words from the Constitution of the United States—"For Ourselves and Our Posterity." For all the flaws of the Founding, no White Nationalist can dispute the beauty of that phrase, nor its relevance to our cause.

Yet as the American Experiment rolls on, even the Constitution is destined to be trampled, as the United States may be the only nation in history where patriotism is defined as the willingness to replace your own citizens.

THE NATURE OF THE AMERICAN POLITY

Any nation, by definition, *excludes*. Some people belong to the political community, and some do not. All nations are reliant to some extent on ethnic kinship. Some admit it, some deny it, but all need it, as the first political communities relied upon blood ties, with extended families developing into tribes. Whether it be an empire or a city-state, any polity needs an ethnic core that can be built upon. A pure "proposition nation" doesn't exist any more than do unicorns—and the fact that some people claim to have seen one or the other makes no difference.

Northern Europeans, for evolutionary, historical, and eventually ideological reasons, are perhaps unique in creating political units ostensibly free of tribalism or ethnic ties. The most popular variant of this is the "social contract" concept that underlies the United States—the government exists solely to protect the "life, liberty, and property" of its citizens, and when it fails to do so, it can be replaced.

The problem with this concept of the state is it ignores

the deeper sources of a state's authority. Most states throughout history have claimed legitimacy from the gods, be it through the Mandate of Heaven, divine right, or sacred blood. But religion itself, of course, partially rests upon a racial or ethnic basis for acceptance.[1]

The nation-state, the most stable political system since the fall of the reactionary and multinational monarchies, derives its authority from its purpose as the political expression of a particular people. Even revolutionary France owed its legitimacy to the idea of the *Patrie* in arms against foreign kings more than some declaration of rights.[2]

Whatever the case, the state becomes worthy of allegiance because it represents something greater than any one person. It is something beyond the people who compromise it, whether it owes its origins to the heavens or to the *Volk*. As Hegel put it, "The march of God in the world, that is what the state is. The basis of the state is the power of reason actualizing itself as will."[3]

Though the Founding Fathers defined their state in classical liberal terms as a necessary institution designed to protect "rights," they still relied upon non-liberal sources of primordial authority. As Jared Taylor outlines in "What the Founders Thought About Race" and other writings, the Founding Fathers took for granted that "only people of European stock could maintain a society in which they would wish to live."[4] Even Thomas Jefferson's egalitarian ideals were grounded in Germanic and Anglo-Saxon conceptions of liberty and active citizenship. His

---

[1] http://www.counter-currents.com/2012/04/the-de-germanization-of-late-american-christianity/

[2] http://en.wikipedia.org/wiki/La_Marseillaise#Lyrics

[3] G. W. F. Hegel, *Philosophy of Right,* § 258.

[4] http://www.npiamerica.org/research/category/what-the-founders-really-thought-about-race/

America was a kind of agrarian *Herrenvolk* republicanism rather than a multicultural democracy.

The Founding Fathers may have talked a lot about equality—but they assumed that America would be a white country of primarily Northern European stock. The purpose of the government was to protect the rights of the people—but it was presupposed that *a people actually existed to be protected*. As John Jay put it in *Federalist Number Two*:

> I have as often taken notice that Providence has been pleased to give this one connected country to one united people—a people descended from the same ancestors, speaking the same language, professing the same religion, attached to the same principles of government, very similar in their manners and customs, and who, by their joint counsels, arms, and efforts, fighting side by side throughout a long and bloody war, have nobly established general liberty and independence.

Unfortunately, the ramifications of this were never really spelled out in the foundation of the state. The existence of the white American people and culture was simply taken for granted. Whatever certain racial laws existed within the country, it was never *explicitly* stated that the United States was to be a country for a particular people. Moreover, economic considerations and the "right" to do whatever one wants with one's own property were held as the highest law even from the beginning. As George Washington put it in a letter looking for workers, "If they are good workmen, they may be of Asia, Africa, or Europe. They may be Mahometans, Jews or Christian of an Sect, or they may be Atheists."[5]

---

[5] http://foundingfathersquotes.blogspot.com/2005/02/

Easy to say when you will only have to command them from your plantation. But what about when they get to vote and become "fellow citizens"? This seems not to have been anticipated.

There were deeper flaws that went beyond race. The Founding Fathers were building on a robust British culture and Western ideas about patriotism, *civitas*, and the state, with a particular focus on the Greek and Roman examples. Unfortunately, they assumed that people would always feel some sense of duty towards the polity. The Founding Fathers seem to believe that because citizens enjoyed "liberty," they would be especially active in defending the state. As Thomas Jefferson said in his first inaugural address, "I believe this . . . the strongest Government on earth. I believe it the only one where every man, at the call of the law, would fly to the standard of the law, and would meet invasions of the public order as his own personal concern."[6]

This is precisely the opposite of what has occurred. As a character says in Harold Covington's *A Mighty Fortress*, "With liberal democracy, you start at a certain level of moral and decent existence and then everything decays from there, kind of like radioactive half-life. The United States started at an exalted level in 1783 and it decayed from that point on."[7] If the premise of the state is to defend "rights," the state merely becomes a utilitarian instrument rather than the source of a sacred authority. Why sacrifice or even care for something that only exists to make sure you can keep your wealth?

Instead of guaranteeing the citizen's devotion to the state, in the long run, the classical liberal state renders

---

george-washington-to-tench-tilghman.html

[6] http://avalon.law.yale.edu/19th_century/jefinau1.asp

[7] http://www.theoccidentalobserver.net/2011/03/harold-covingtons-northwest-quartet/

citizenship meaningless. If it is not based on sacred duty, ethnicity, or shared culture, it is simply a legal and (more importantly) economic instrument. As such, "loyalty" is moot—the country you want to "belong" to is the country that offers you the best deal. And as the franchise inevitably expands, the services and programs offered by the state do as well. Politicians bribe the voters with their own money—except for those who can also donate to their re-election coffers, who receive special bribes of their own.

The result is that the state is most responsive to those constituencies that offer the least to the national community. Slowly democracy transforms into kakistocracy—rule by the worst. A welfare-dependent minority that votes as part of a bloc is an important part of a politician's winning coalition. A white suburban office drone with a mortgage is just a *kulak* to be drained for resources. More than that, those who receive the most from the state seem to be those who contribute the least to the common good.

The country can trade off its accumulated cultural strengths for a long time, but not forever. Eventually, civic virtue collapses. Mark Steyn in *After America* quotes Tom Wolfe, who notes that historically most people don't live for themselves, but see themselves (even if unconsciously) as "part of a great biological stream" binding the lives of their ancestors, children, and even their neighbors. But in a modern democracy, Steyn writes, "You don't need to make material sacrifices: the state takes care of all that. You don't need to have children. And you certainly don't need to die for king and country." As he put it elsewhere, "An army has to wage war on behalf of something real. For better or worse, 'king and country' is real, and so, mostly for worse, are the tribal loyalties of Africa's blood-drenched civil wars."[8]

If there is "nothing to kill or die for," there is nothing to

---

[8] http://www.steynonline.com/4132/too-big-to-win

live for either. The result is that just like religion in the modern world, patriotism is a lifestyle choice—what country's passport you hold is only slightly more important than what soft drink you prefer or whether you support Xbox or PlayStation.[9] Indeed, a person's preferred gaming system may be a greater subject of emotional attachment than their supposed country.

When you are a deracinated individual living in a society that upholds deracinated individualism as its highest virtue, you have no stake in the survival of that society. And on the rare occasions the society tries to harness its people to a collective purpose, the "citizens" look around and realize they have nothing in common with one another, not even interests. Why should they care?

AN EMPTY AMERICA FOR BOTH LEFT & RIGHT

In the Age of Obama, progressives have grown increasingly comfortable openly defending government as the "only we thing all belong to," in the Democratic National Committee's phrase. This idea is infuriating to the Beltway Right. But conservatives themselves are slowly reaching their final form as economists who make their free market fundamentalism palatable with a belief in "American Exceptionalism."[10]

What is American Exceptionalism? Even its leading proponents find it hard to define. Addressing the concept, James Kirkpatrick writes:

> American Exceptionalism can variously mean that America is immune to the laws of history, or more virtuous, or more capitalist, or more powerful than everyone else. Sometimes it is supposed to

---

[9] https://www.youtube.com/watch?v=p2cAQnpCpAk
[10] http://knowyourmeme.com/memes/this-isnt-even-my-final-form

mean all of these things at once.

Occasionally, Republican politicians seem to believe that American Exceptionalism means that America must always act independently and be at the forefront of any global situation, simply for its own sake. Having abandoned racial, religious, and cultural forms of identity, and with the Constitution "no serious threat to our system of government" (in Joe Sobran's phrase), a nonsensical tautology is all the true believers in America have left. America is different, they say, because it is America.[11]

In policy terms, it doesn't say what America actually *is*—what policies it pursues, what the structure of government is, or even what people make it up. What matters is that it still calls itself the United States and is therefore worthy of the same attachment and sacrifice as the Anglo-Saxon America of 1783. American conservatism is a cargo cult masquerading as a political philosophy.

Ultimately, both sides in mainstream American politics are united in defining the country as a cultureless and raceless entity. To the Left, being a consumer of government services makes you an American—indeed, it's the only thing that makes you an American. A client of the welfare state is far more patriotic than some sad old rube like Cliven Bundy—who is a "traitor," to use Harry Reid's phrase.[12] Thus, Vice President Joe Biden, the Democrats' go-to white male token[13] for the rubes, says of illegal immigrants occupying the nation's territory that "I believe

---

[11] http://www.npiamerica.org/the-national-policy-institute/category/doomed-to-exceptionalism

[12] http://www.counter-currents.com/2014/04/fear-of-a-white-rancher/

[13] http://www.vdare.com/articles/biden-ryan-and-the-unrepresented-white-working-class

they're already American citizens."[14] Notably, the white working man's champion made these remarks to the Hispanic Chamber of Commerce.

As for the Republicans, they define Americanism as contributing to the economy—preferably in the form of cheap labor, so as to increase the profits of donors. Thus, the flagship magazine of American conservatism, *National Review*, graces us with an article entitled "Immigration, America's Advantage."[15] One author is Lee Habeeb, a talk radio executive who makes his living telling your typical *Lumpenkonservative* what he wants to hear and finding others to do the same.

The other is Mike Leven, who is apparently a noted conservative scholar even though his day job is serving as an executive for Las Vegas Sands. His boss is Sheldon Adelson, a wealthy Jewish donor who has more influence on American conservatives than you ever will. Adelson, you will be happy to know, funds[16] and supports the "Birthright" program designed to cultivate loyalty to his ethnostate and wants a fence around "our country" (by which he means Israel).[17] In America, like his underling Leven, he is one of the leading voices for amnesty.[18] The charge of dual loyalty would be unfair—because dual loyalty would be a dramatic improvement.

The article itself is interesting because it directly ad-

---

[14] http://thehill.com/blogs/blog-briefing-room/news/201972-biden-illegal-immigrants-already-americans

[15] http://www.nationalreview.com/article/376523/immigration-americas-advantage-lee-habeeb-and-mike-leven

[16] http://www.jta.org/2013/05/23/news-opinion/united-states/adelsons-donate-40-million-to-birthright

[17] http://articles.latimes.com/2013/may/28/world/la-fg-wn-sheldon-adelson-israel-20130528

[18] http://www.vdare.com/articles/sheldon-adelson-buys-amnesty-from-gop-establishment-but-will-rank-and-file-agree

dresses population decline and even ethnic demographics. For example:

> Take Russia. According to the United Nations, its adult population will fall from 90 million today to 20 million by the end of the century. Eighty percent of the population of the Russian Federation are ethnic Russians, but fertility is higher among Central Asian Muslim minorities. Some experts predict a Muslim majority in Russia by 2040. This past year, more babies were aborted in Russia than were born.

While not directly stated, it is obviously implied that a majority-Muslim Russia isn't really Russia and that to survive, the country has to not just increase its population, but increase its ethnic Russian population. The reference to abortion following the prediction of the Muslim majority implies that the country would not be facing this threat if the practice wasn't so prevalent.

Japan and Europe are also said to share the fate of demographic decline, through Muslim immigration is curiously not mentioned as something worth considering in Western Europe.

In contrast:

> America's secret weapon on the all-important population front is our immigrant advantage. It's our immigrant population that has kept America from falling over the demographic cliff of late. Today, there are roughly 38 million people in the U.S. who were born somewhere else; two-thirds of them are here legally.
>
> "Consider that just four million babies are born annually in the U.S.," Jonathan Last wrote in *The Weekly Standard* last year. "If you strip these immigrants—and their relatively high fertility rates—

from our population profile, America suddenly looks an awful lot like continental Europe."

Not asked is who these "Americans" are. As the above states, most of the groups with a higher fertility rate come from the immigrant population. What difference does it make if "American" population growth is coming from people who have nothing in common with the rest of the country except standing on the same piece of dirt? And why does it matter when we are talking about Russia, but it suddenly doesn't when we are talking about America?

The answer is that there is no America. There's just an economy. The remainder of the article simply outlines the ways that immigrants allegedly help the economy. Laughing is the only way to keep from crying when reading the arguments and normative claims that follow.

To take just one example, America is "Scrooge-like" because the government doesn't distribute enough H-1B visas for skilled workers. The spectacle of gambling executives lecturing Americans for being "Scrooge-like" for *opposing* lower wages speaks for itself.

Eventually, we are told, "America should do more than simply cherry-pick from the world's 'best and brightest' workers. We should increase our numbers of 'unskilled' immigrants, too."

Ignoring the disastrous economic consequences of mass immigration and instead praising it as a blessing is bad enough. But what we have here is a case of almost religious fundamentalism—as if anyone can seriously believe America's greatest weakness is a lack of unskilled peasants from the Third World.

But they aren't just cheap labor. In fact, they're better than you. Habeeb and Leven write:

No one takes a berth in steerage because he heard that in America the government gives you stuff. It takes courage to leave your country and cross an ocean. Most immigrants do it not for themselves but for their families. That kind of selflessness and risk-taking is a perfect American skill set, perfectly reflecting our national character.

Some minor points. First, notice the reference to the "berth in steerage," meant to call up hallowed memories of Ellis Island and plucky, hard-working immigrants coming from Europe.[19] Apparently we are expected to believe that after thorough processing, contemporary immigrants will set up fruit stands while their children play stickball.

Of course, what we have today are overwhelmingly non-white immigrants who cross the Southern border illegally with the benign indifference of those who rule us and are supposed to protect us. Once they arrive in their new country, illegal immigrants from Mexico regard the United States with contempt and loathing, unable to keep from shouting anti-American slogans even while marching for amnesty. The majority of the immigrants in this country never "crossed an ocean," just the Rio Grande. But Leven's ancestors did, and we have to pay for it for all eternity.

Secondly, the vast majority of immigrants to any country throughout history "did it for their families." Why this fact is supposed to have an impact on public policy is unknown. However, this current group of immigrants is probably *less* likely to "do it for their families" than any other group in history. A not insignificant percentage of Hispanic illegals are sneaking across the border by themselves and then either entrusting their children to a coyote or simply expecting them to get to America alone. Another common occurrence is children being dumped in the US by parents who don't want them—another triumph of

---

[19] http://takimag.com/article/mythos_and_blood_steve_sailer/

Hispanic family values.

The results are predictable as "the children" and future "DREAMers" so beloved by the media are raped, abused, or even killed.[20] The media is largely silent about these crimes, or finds a way to blame it on whites. After all, it's not as if something really bad happened to them—like a white guy calling them a racial slur. What's being murdered compared to the "microaggression" of a Southern accent?

But the point here is to appeal to American conservatives. American conservatives like "families," immigrants (mostly) like their "families," therefore, conservatives should like immigrants. Hey, they are just like us!

Third, it's simply not true that immigrants don't know that the government "gives you stuff." In fact, you can track migration patterns of non-whites in the United States based on the generosity of the welfare available, as the residents of Maine[21] and Minnesota[22] suddenly swamped by Somalis are finding out. Immigrants are far more likely to use means-tested welfare programs than non-immigrants.[23] And the American government actually is partnering with Mexican consulates to make sure Mexican immigrants in the United States receive EBT payments—paid for, of course, by American taxpayers.[24] If an immigrant hasn't heard that the American government doesn't just "give you stuff," it's not for the Obama re-

---

[20] http://vdare.com/articles/obama-s-illegal-alien-magnet-kills-another-child

[21] http://www.vdare.com/posts/in-lewiston-maine-somalis-keep-coming

[22] http://super-economy.blogspot.com/2010/09/dont-believe-hype-somali-immigration-to.html

[23] http://www.fairus.org/issue/immigration-and-welfare

[24] http://www.limitstogrowth.org/articles/2013/04/26/washington-partners-with-mexico-to-deliver-food-stamps-to-mexican-illegals/

gime's lack of trying.

But there's a bigger issue to all this. Implicit in every-thing the authors are saying is the idea that Americans exist to serve an abstraction called the economy. Indeed, the greater the "skill set" of each American, the more American they are. We will exceed Russia, Japan, and "Old Europe" precisely because we are willing to replace our-selves in order to keep our welfare state functioning and our GDP growing.

It's not entirely true that American conservatives are without a sense of race. After all, John McCain channeled a kind of Bizarro Miguel Serrano when he said, "Anyone who is afraid that somehow our culture will be anything but enriched by fresh blood and culture, in my view, has a distorted view of history and has a pessimistic view of our future."[25] Jeb Bush brags about the "fertility" of the new Hispanic America he is trying to create, and cuckold con-servatives like Matt Lewis actually gloat about whites "not having babies." However, in any of these cases, if whites actually *were* to start having babies or the American polity implemented pro-natal policies, can anyone doubt these same people would call it "un-American"?

Perhaps the authors are right when they say "selfless-ness" is key to the American national character, but not in the way they meant. Presumably if every single American were replaced by a more productive worker tomorrow, "we" still would have triumphed somehow, as Americans.

TEAM AMERICA

In the eyes of its fiercest conservative defenders, Amer-ica is a team. Anyone can buy the jersey—even if it is made overseas by coolie labor. The country provides peo-ple with an opportunity to make money with fewer re-

---

[25] http://www.vdare.com/articles/exposing-matt-lewis-pro-mass-immigration-motives-and-canards

straints than anywhere else, and that's it. But what else do you need? As the satirical program *South Park*'s Stan Marsh said in the first episode after 9/11, "America's our home . . . it's our team." To which Kyle replies, "Go America. And go Broncos."[26]

At the risk of overanalyzing a cartoon, this is basically how most people think of the country. It's all they have left. The problem of course is that a real nation or tribe isn't a team—it's part of your very identity, something as deep and important as your family or sex. Of course, since both of those are "social constructs" now, it's probably not surprising that a nation is too.

Unfortunately for the country, no one else has this abstract idea of patriotism except white Americans, especially conservatives. To take the metaphor a bit further, while white Americans fantasize about the global standing of some abstraction based on "ideals" and "values," their non-white fellow citizens can't support "Team USA" even when it comes to sports, as the US Soccer team playing in Los Angeles found out.[27] Non-whites have their ethnostates and their real homelands. Only white conservatives are left with their proposition nation.

The Left is more honest. It at least admits that there is a historic American nation of European Americans. The Left just hates it. The new America is an egalitarian empire where membership is defined as fealty to the government. Indeed, in the Age of Obama it is the Left that is adopting the "love it or leave it" rhetoric of the Vietnam-era American Right. Criticizing the President's new health care law is "unpatriotic," after all.

In both cases, your loyalty to the country is defined as

---

[26] https://www.youtube.com/watch?v=lFYcXi5a1Lo

[27] http://www.theblaze.com/stories/2011/06/26/disgrace-u-s-soccer-team-faces-boos-and-spanish-language-ceremony-in-loss-to-mexico-in-los-angeles/

your loyalty to an abstraction—either in propping up a government or an economy that we somehow belong to. Neither Left nor Right thinks the country should be connected to any particular group of people. It is simply *there*, and we happen to be on it.

The racial ramifications are easy to spell out. American Indians become "Native Americans" who are more authentically American than the British settlers of Jamestown or Plymouth. A slave "built" the country in a more substantial way than a Washington, Jefferson, or Madison. And Mexicans in the American Southwest have a greater claim to the American story than white settlers moving west—after all, Mexicans can say "the border crossed us, we didn't cross the border."

How often in the immigration debate does a Leftist make what he thinks is the knockout argument that America "belongs" to the Indians—forgetting of course, that, in George Lincoln Rockwell's phrase, "America did not exist until the coming of the white man."[28] But you can't say that if your country is just a geographic expression.

The result is a polity indifferent to its ethnic core and founding stock. It can replace and dispossess the people who created it and somehow operate on the assumption that it is the same place. More importantly, even the people who are being replaced and dispossessed will think it is the same place. Instead of the country that the Framers created "for Ourselves and Our Posterity," what we have is a country that belongs to everyone except the people who founded it. We don't have a Fatherland or a Motherland— just a "homeland."

Ironically, to flip around what Edward Wilson said in *The Good Shepherd*, it's everyone else who has the United

---

[28] http://www.counter-currents.com/2013/03/rockwell-as-conservative/

States of America. Whites are just visiting.

What is most frustrating about this is whatever high idealism is used to justify the universalistic vision of Left or Right, in the end what drives policy is the basest materialism of the worst members of society. The classical liberal vision has ultimately triumphed because the American state is a resource to be exploited by the individual—either through government benefits or the subsidization of corporations and cheap labor. A classical liberal's protest that his vision was of "limited government" changes nothing about the inevitability of the sprawling EBT democracy his vision has spawned.

The American system is an engine of degradation for everyone involved—and the fuel it relies upon is the misguided idealism of those white Americans who keep feeding into the system. Absent radical change, it will continue running—until it has fully replaced the very people it relies upon.

Ultimately, we must return to first principles. What is the nation? And who compromises it? White Nationalists have an answer. The triumphs of the historic American nation are the product of the European Americans who built it. That population must awaken to itself and become a people. And once it is aware of itself as a people, it must seize a state for itself, rooted in Primordial Tradition and racial reality rather than phony Enlightenment slogans ignored by the same people who put them to paper.

The legacy of achievement of the United States of America will belong to the rising state. But the failed classical liberal ideology must be rejected at every level. Our nation and our people are one and the same—and it belongs to Ourselves and Our Posterity, alone.

Counter-Currents/*North American New Right*,
May 2, 2014

DINESH D'SOUZA'S *AMERICA*

There's no easier way to make a living than as a nonwhite activist in the American conservative movement.[1] Simply offer well-meaning whites the nectar of racial absolution and say you care about their country, and they will throw money at you no matter what else you do. The recognized master of this unique form of hucksterism is Dinesh D'Souza, who specializes in capitalizing on implicit white identity while making sure it is funneled into ideological dead ends.[2]

D'Souza's documentary *America* is subtitled *Imagine a World Without Her*. It begins with an alternate history where George Washington is killed in battle. Several supposedly negative scenarios are outlined, from a Southern victory in the War of Northern Aggression to Germany winning World War II.

But instead of exploring these, D'Souza spends the bulk of the movie defending America against the charges that it is racist and exploitative. He concocts a theory that America has transcended a "conquest ethic" in favor of a production ethic of wealth creation. D'Souza thus smoothly transforms the race-driven hatred of anti-American Leftists into an economic dispute over resources.

D'Souza ends the movie with an exploration of Saul Alinsky's career, which was defined by "rubbing raw the resentments of the people" in order to create socialist revolution. D'Souza gives us a hilarious scene where the extremely Jewish Alinsky leers at the residents of a white

---

[1] http://www.vdare.com/articles/brc-black-run-conservatism-vs-gap-generic-american-party

[2] http://www.vdare.com/articles/dinesh-dsouza-the-right-enemies-but-the-wrong-thesis

middle-class neighborhood, gleefully pondering how to ruin their lives. However, D'Souza leaves aside the racial element of Alinsky's shaming tactics and his identification of the "white" middle class as the enemy, instead transforming Alinsky's entire motivation simply into "socialism."

Wave the flag, roll credits, vote Republican.

From the perspective of interest and entertainment, D'Souza squanders the promising premise of the film. A history of the world without America could have been genuinely provocative. However, he can't do that because what his Left-wing critics hate is not "America" but the white people who created her. He has to transform the visceral racial politics of American history into a policy dispute over Obamacare. That's how the scam known as Conservatism Inc. operates.

But there's a deeper question here for Traditionalists. All of D'Souza's "charges" against America come from the Left. Perhaps the film that needs to be made is a critique of America from the Right. *America, Imagine a World Without Her: From Our Eyes.*

FOUR CHARGES AGAINST AMERICA

"The United States represents the *reductio ad absurdum* of the negative and the most senile aspects of Western civilization."

—Julius Evola, *Civiltà Americana*

1. America replaced tradition and identity with equality.

Is there any phrase in history that has been more destructive in its effects, unlimited in its implications, and self-evidently false in its content than "all men are created equal"?

As our leaders never tire of telling us, America is an

idea, not a nation, and the idea is that human beings are born with certain unalienable rights. Government exists only to protect the rights of individuals, leaving them free to pursue the American Dream—which usually consists of working pointless jobs in order to buy more disposable goods in the Lockean shopping mall we call a country.

But the American Revolution was a mistake.[3] The result was not a free nation, but a random collection of rootless, powerless, deracinated consumers ruled more despotically by financiers and the media than any peasant under George III. The ideological foundation of America was rotten from the beginning.[4] What's worse is that even as Americans move away from traditional American "patriotism," they believe ever-more frantically that more democracy and equality is the answer. Sarah Albers notes in *The American Conservative* that recent polling shows:

> Young Americans are emphatically committed to the principles upon which America was founded, but will sometimes reject the country itself as well as the wisdom and history embodied in its establishment. It is fealty to an idea, not loyalty to a nation, that they profess.[5]

America is playing out to its logical conclusion. The horrible truth of America's founding ideology is that it is both the problem and the only permitted solution. There can never be a society that is equal, free, or "happy."

---

[3] http://www.amerika.org/politics/why-the-american-revolution-was-a-mistake/

[4] http://www.youtube.com/watch?v=DSSKSK1ZHdI

[5] http://www.theamericanconservative.com/america-the-abstracted/

D'Souza is fond of quoting Alexis de Tocqueville in his film but leaves out his observation that "Americans are so enamored of equality that they would rather be equal in slavery than unequal in freedom." Joseph Sobran once said that conservatives should ask liberals if there was any society in which *they* would be conservative. He missed the point. The endless march towards the impossible ideal is the American story, an absurd quest doomed to failure and destined only to lead to a continual destruction of everything worthwhile. The only escape is to say from the beginning that the ideal itself is absurd.

Had the forces of King George III succeeded, perhaps this sinister specter of "rights" would not have been unleashed upon the world. We can imagine a world where Edmund Burke's "age of sophisters, economists, and calculators" that heralded the end of the "glory of Europe" was postponed, if not prevented. And while a monarch still reigns in the Court of St. James, it is but hollow symbolism. The annihilation of the aristocratic principle heralded by Yorktown has transformed the royal houses of Europe into tourist attractions for decadent democracies rather than bulwarks of Tradition.

Unfortunately, the colonials were saved by Louis XVI of France, who—foreshadowing the West's entire history over the next few centuries—would be slain by the very egalitarian forces he unleashed in the interest of petty power politics.

2. America destroyed Europe.

America defined itself as a rejection of the Old World with its kings, traditions, and nations.

Occasionally, this was even taken to the extent of dreaming of an anti-European bloc in opposition to the Continent. As Thomas Jefferson put it in 1820, "Nothing is so important as that America shall separate herself from the systems of Europe, and establish one of her own."

Jefferson's primary concern was keeping aloof from what he called the "ferocious and sanguinary" contests of Europe, but this was more than just policy. It reflected a core element of American nationalism, which defined itself as a negation, the "anti-Europe." To this day, "European" is a slur among the "patriots" of the American Right.[6] And this eventually manifested itself in an *interventionist* foreign policy, rather than the nonintervention of the early Republic. As Michael O'Meara, commenting on the work of Francis Parker Yockey, put it:

> During the 19th century, the rising commercial and business classes, communicating vessels of the liberal ethos, allied with the cosmopolitan capitalism of the British Empire and the ascending economic might of America's new low-church empire—an alliance ideologically arrayed under the banner of "Anglo-Saxonism" and implicitly opposed to continental Europeans attached to Listian economics, landed property, authority, and tradition . . .
>
> Though the "true America," transplant of Europe, shared her destiny, Yockey believed modern liberal America had become an anti-Europe endeavoring not only to subjugate, occupy, and oppress her, but to destroy her unique heritage of blood and spirit.[7]

---

[6] http://www.radixjournal.com/journal/2014/7/15/the-hope-of-europeanization

[7] http://www.counter-currents.com/2014/07/america-imagine-a-world-without-her/%20http:/www.counter-currents.com/2010/06/the-death-of-francis-parker-yockey/

This eventually expressed itself in a remarkably consistent opposition to European attempts to re-establish a link with Tradition. In what Revilo Oliver termed the "Crusade to Save the Soviet" of World War II, America ensured that Eastern Europe would be handed over to the Soviet Union—and then turned its attention to dismantling what Western European empires and white settler states remained.

The anti-Communist Cold War that followed, rather than a jihad against the global Left, made racial egalitarianism a strategic necessity and established it as an American moral principle as the United States battled the Soviet Union around the world.[8] Ironically, it is the United States that has emerged as the great champion of cultural Marxism even as post-Cold War Russia moves in a more conservative direction, raising the question for the American Right whether they actually lost the Cold War.[9]

Through culture, through economics, and through military interventions like that against Serbia, the United States is committed to preventing the rise of a truly European Europe. In the words of General Wesley Clark during the NATO offensive to secure Muslim Kosovo, "There is no place in modern Europe for ethnically pure states. That's a 19th-century idea and we are trying to transition into the 21st century, and we are going to do it with multi-ethnic states."

It's the American idea of a deracinated state founded upon human rights that triumphed in postwar Europe. It's that idea that needs to be destroyed if Europe is to be liberated. And the only thing those Americans who are

---

[8] http://www.counter-currents.com/2011/02/the-cold-war-on-whites/

[9] http://www.unz.com/article/how-the-left-won-the-cold-war/

truly loyal to Western culture may be able to do today is prevent America from attacking, bombing, and occupying Europe if she rediscovers herself.

In the world without America, Europe would have remained true to herself. The mother continent of the West would not be faced with the choice of being either a soulless museum or a conquered province of the Dar al-Islam. And the identity of Western Man would not have been deconstructed in order to make the world safe for McDonald's. Which brings us to . . .

3. America replaced culture with consumerism.

One of D'Souza's main points is that capitalism has created more wealth and has lifted more people out of poverty than any other economic system. He points to nations like India and China as examples of the power of the free market.

It's easy to say that vulgar American materialism is jeopardizing spiritual values, even though it's true. Most people have little time for spiritual values if they can't provide for their families. The problem is that D'Souza's thesis fails on its own terms.

The rising Asian Tigers that will dominate the economy of the near future follow a nationalist form of state capitalism. It's easy enough to say centrally planned Soviet Communism is a proven failure. It's far harder to say that American-style free trade and debt-driven financial capitalism is somehow superior to that practiced by the other economic powers, especially considering how different our current system is from the original "American System" of tariffs, internal improvements, manufacturing, and high wages.[10]

The modern American outlook on economics holds

---

[10] http://en.wikipedia.org/wiki/American_System_%28 economic_plan%29

that the nation exists to serve the economy, rather than the economy exists to serve the nation. For example, *all* employment growth since 2000 in the United States has gone to benefit immigrants.[11] From a nationalist perspective, this means that Americans have essentially been treading water for all those years. However, from an American financier's perspective, an abstraction called the "economy" is growing, and therefore, the country is on the right track.

Instead of examining issues like quality of life, the cost of raising a family, or whether employees enjoy job security, the American financial system focuses on the all-important issue of growing GDP, propping up the system through ever-increasing debt and using the dollar's status as the "reserve currency" to just keep printing more money to keep the charade going.

The result is a something that cannot really be called a "culture"—just a market selling junk. The American economic system prioritizes spending over investment, consumption over creation, and cheap labor over efficiency and quality. While the "economy" is growing, the quality of life for most Americans is decreasing as living in a "nice" (white) neighborhood requires absurd amounts of resources. What a one-income household could do on a union job not long ago now costs $130,000 a year.[12]

But that's not the real crime. The real crime is not just that everything is a commodity, it's that everything is a cheap throwaway commodity. Everything is disposable. Nothing is sacred, and everything is shoddy.

The government subsidizes harmful junk food while raiding families that produce their own milk or grow

---

[11] http://www.vdare.com/posts/shock-study-cis-drudge-and-nro-repeat-what-vdare-com-has-been-saying-for-years

[12] http://www.usatoday.com/story/money/personalfinance/2014/07/04/american-dream/11122015/

their own food.[13] Irresponsible sexual behavior is rewarded and traditional families punished. High-paying jobs
are actually targeted for destruction by the government,
the better for them to be replaced by foreign helot labor.
It's as if our rulers read Marx's taunt that capitalism
turns even family life into brutal economic calculation
and thought, "That sounds like a great idea."

What was the alternative? The organic society, the
Volksgemeinschaft where the economy serves the nation
and culture. Economic policy is formulated to improve
the quality of life for the community and promote the
upward development of the race. Efficiency, quality, and
beauty are priorities. Companies invest in workers and
are tied to particular communities—a system which continues today in Germany, the powerhouse of the European Union.[14] Instead of an economy that subsidizes the
worst in people, we could have had something which
promotes the best.

But we didn't. And when every community is destroyed, every worker ground into the dirt, and every ne-
oliberal policy prized as holy writ, what is the result? A
nation of unhappy consumers, addicted to prescription
drugs, who build their lives around the accumulation of
plastic junk. What's more, even though materialism is all
that American culture has to offer, somehow, everyone is
broke and in debt—as is the country itself.[15]

---

[13] http://communities.washingtontimes.com/
neighborhood/reading-ingredients-tales-health-conscious-
mom/2011/jun/18/film-exposes-government-raids-family-
farms/

[14] http://www.vdare.com/articles/democrat-suggest-
immigration-patriots-should-support-patriotic-capitalism-
german-style-code

[15] http://www.nationalreview.com/articles/333116/edge-
abyss-mark-steyn

4. America destroys the people who built her.

Having destroyed the European culture that created her, America is now fulfilling her destiny as an eternal revolutionary state by eating her own children. Even as this is written, the President of the United States is ignoring his responsibility to enforce the law to gleefully ship in immigrants from Central America. Some are gang members, some are carrying diseases,[16] and none have anything to offer the United States except the open hand of a beggar or the clenched fist of an enemy.[17]

The effects of America's own government are indistinguishable from that of military conquest by a foreign enemy. But millions of Americans support their own displacement because they see it as the fulfillment of their own national mission. And they are right.

If America is an "idea," and the pursuit of a "better life" is all that matters, why not let in the needy? After all, they would have a better life here. We won't, of course, but it's not about us. White people have no particular claim to this land—which is, after all, simply an administrative unit for the management of the economy and the protection of "rights"—so why not let everyone in?

The obvious retort is that the historic American nation and its accomplishments was a *European* creation. In the immortal words of Sam Francis:

> The civilization that we as whites created in Europe and America could not have developed apart from the genetic endowments of the creating people, nor is there any reason to believe that the civi-

---

[16] http://www.vdare.com/posts/border-patrol-agent-contracts-bacterial-pneumonia-from-illegal-alien-processing

[17] http://www.counter-currents.com/2014/07/conscience-as-a-weapon/

lization can be successfully transmitted to a different people.[18]

However, the American ideology is not capable of making that argument. Self-conscious American patriots lack the vocabulary for a defense of their national existence, identified as it is with explicitly universal ideas. Thus America is the Spenglerian cycle of nations in accelerated form. The hardy pioneers, conquerors, and settlers swiftly surrender their moral right to existence and collapse into decadence. And why shouldn't they? After all, America isn't a people and a history—it's a flag and a piece of paper.

CONCLUSION

These are the charges against America from the Traditionalist Right. And the truth of the indictment can be seen in the world around us—the world America built, the world that is killing us.

D'Souza loves this country because it is the greatest defender of the classical liberalism that makes people like him possible. It is also the greatest enemy of white survival, and the greatest engine of white degradation. These two truths are complementary because when all is said and done, America, like D'Souza, is a scam. But every con has its end.

The only way white Americans can survive is without America, and it begins by "imagining a world without her." It's easy if you try.

Counter-Currents/*North American New Right*,
July 17, 2014

---

[18] Samuel Francis, "Why Race Matters," *American Renaissance*, September 1994, http://www.amren.com/ar/1994/09/index.html

RACE:
THE FIRST PRINCIPLE

It's a common dodge for opponents of White Nationalism, even sympathetic opponents, to charge that "race
isn't enough" to build a society. This misses the point. Of
course "whiteness" in and of itself doesn't solve all problems—although a society solely composed of even the
most degraded elements of our own people would be far
preferable to the current embarrassment we call a country.

Race is superior to any other foundational principle,
including religion, ideology, or economics as the basis of a
society. A sophisticated understanding of race is in and of
itself sufficient to ensure the survival and perpetuation of
a society. In the end, this is the only test that really matters.

At the most basic level, the physical existence of the
people has to be guaranteed before anything else can be
considered. Economic recession, military occupation, dis-
ease, and political repression can pass with time—all are
temporary if the folk remains intact. As the Afrikaner Resistance Movement of South Africa wrote in its founding
principles, "As long as the race remains biologically pure,
the possibility and probability of rebirth and resistance is
always there."[1]

Race is the key building block of any real community
and the farthest meaningful grouping to which we can
give our loyalty. We know that genetic similarity and kinship patterns affect our behavior every day, even in ways
we don't expect. We know that children are race con-

---

[1] http://www.amren.com/features/2013/05/when-
patriotism-meets-conservatism/

scious as early as nine months.[2] We know that people are mentally healthier in ethnically homogeneous societies.[3] We know diversity destroys social trust, eventually even within members of the same ethnic group.[4] The ancients knew this, and modern science confirms it.

Our society's frantic efforts to escape these truths gives us the farce that passes for a public debate in a multiethnic democracy, when major magazines can publish breathless cover stories like "Is Your Baby Racist?" without irony. We set up entire social systems and ideologies at odds with our most basic instincts and wonder why the world seems to have lost its mind.

Race is the hidden foundation of the supposed pillars of society and morality. Religion is the most obvious example. Haitian, French, and Chinese Catholics all submit to the Magisterium, but it would be foolish to speak of them as belong to the same "religion" in any meaningful sense or sharing the same experience of the divine. A people's understanding of the gods, the relationship between faith and the state, and the practice of worship owe more to traditions ingrained deep within the folk than any defined creed. As James Russell described in *The Germanization of Early Medieval Christianity*, "Conversion is as much a bargaining process as a conquest, with the indigenous people transforming creed even as it changes them."[5] These expressions may be rooted in the genes themselves, something even more primordial than thousands of years

---

[2] http://www.amren.com/news/2012/05/babies-develop-racist-traits-aged-nine-months-before-coming-into-contact-with-other-races/

[3] http://m.bjp.rcpsych.org/content/201/4/282.full

[4] http://www.vdare.com/articles/robert-putnam-diversity-is-our-destruction

[5] James C. Russell, *The Germanization of Early Medieval Christianity: A Sociohistorical Approach to Religious Transformation* (New York: Oxford University Press, 1994), ch. 2.

of history.

The problem is that absent race and a folk conscious-ness, the faith becomes an alienating, even hostile force against its own people.

Witness devout Muslims destroying priceless Islamic shrines on the grounds they are deviations from "true" Islam, Cromwell's Puritans banning the "pagan" festival of Christmas, or Orthodox Jews refusing to defend Israel, preferring to study Torah all day and sponge off welfare. In the United States at the ground level, there is no force more powerful in the effort to dispossess white Americans through mass non-white immigration than the Christian churches, with the possible exception of the government itself. Of course, absent their core population and cultural ties, these same churches (especially the mainline Protestant denominations) will shrivel up and die. After all, what real impact does Lutheranism as a creed have on America today, other than afflicting us with more Soma-lis?

This alienating process is all but inevitable as impulses that enable continued collective existence clash with sui-cidal moral principles. Insofar as a universalistic religion survives amongst a people, it survives through hypocrisy.

Political ideology is another red herring. A comparison between North and South Korea should be sufficient to prove that ideology matters. However, even in North Ko-rea, it's an ideology of thinly veiled racial nationalism that serves as the indispensable support for what would other-wise be a doomed system. In multicultural democracies, repeated studies show that voters are unwilling to support social welfare programs if they are perceived as supporting foreign groups.[6] It's no coincidence that American con-servatism is characterized by marshaling white resent-

---

[6] http://www.vdare.com/articles/diversity-is-strength-its-also-the-worst-sort-of-welfare-state

ment against non-white welfare recipients—though conservatives will hasten to explain it has "nothing to do with race."[7] As Lee Kuan Yew of Singapore put it, "In multiracial societies, you don't vote in accordance with your economic interests and social interests, you vote in accordance with race and religion."[8]

Of course, the defining characteristic of the modern era is economism, the reduction of all human interaction to the purely monetary. It was Marx who first highlighted this reductionist aspect of capitalism, the destruction of the traditional social order.[9] While Marx sneered that this was simply the stripping away of sentiment, today's liberals (classical or otherwise) miss entirely the undercurrent of despair and tragedy. Instead, they proclaim they are *sui generis*, proudly renouncing any unchosen commitments to family, race, religion, nation, or morality. In the new world, only what a person can create in terms of currency matters.

Such a world rebuts itself. The modern consumerist America of depressed, drug-addicted denizens frantically rutting and intoxicating themselves to avoid suicide is hardly a Galt's Gulch of liberated supermen.

A degraded culture, broken families, and a flourishing marketplace that traffics in human misery are not worth defending. It's a life of consummate meaninglessness.

However, the economist premise fails even on its own terms. Even a casual glance around the Western world reveals the massive financial fraud and manipulation required to keep the system limping along. In real economic

---

[7] http://www.vdare.com/articles/fuel-for-the-furnace-conservatism-inc-and-sam-francis

[8] http://isteve.blogspot.com/2005/08/lee-kwan-yew-on-democracy-vs.html

[9] http://www.traditionalbritain.org/content/marx-contra-marx-conservative-interpretation-communist-manifesto

terms, the quality of life has not increased for decades, even in the midst of dramatic technological progress.[10]

A true libertarian could object that all this is because we don't have "true" capitalism, "the unknown ideal." The absence of any "truly" free society in all of human history that meets their standards would seem to suggest that this fantastical ideology doesn't have much basis in fact. One can't simply beg the question by positing an abstract utopia and then wishing the real world out of existence.

But even if we dismiss the objection from practicality, libertarianism fails on its own terms. Large-scale investments in infrastructure, conscious efforts to ameliorate class divisions, productivity-based economics, and deliberate maintenance of high-wage levels and a tight labor market to spur technological innovation are objectively superior policies from the standpoint of economic productivity.

Even if we dismiss this objection as well, a "perfect" libertarianism still requires preventing the lower classes from obtaining state power, presumably through some sort of hyperactive authoritarianism in the manner of Pinochet. Furthermore, the capitalist desire for short-term cheap labor would inevitably lead to the replacement of skilled workers by low-IQ helots that would degrade overall economic performance while increasing social obligations. A society of pure "freedom" inevitably becomes a rigid hierarchy that requires denying vast sections of the population a political outlet in order to maintain the system. It's no surprise that the open borders faction of the American conservative movement replies to this objection by just wishing it out of existence, simply positing that low-IQ Hispanic laborers will suddenly transform into WASPs over the course of a generation.

---

[10] http://economix.blogs.nytimes.com/2012/10/22/the-uncomfortable-truth-about-american-wages/

What happens is that race reasserts itself even in nominally economist societies. Even if you cut low-IQ non-whites off from having a political voice, even if you strip any consideration of race or culture from policy, race will assert itself in housing patterns, business relationships, and consumer behavior below the surface, even under pure libertarianism. Without civil rights laws and the state-run egalitarian bureaucracy, a libertarian society would undoubtedly be a more openly racialist society, despite its individualist principles. The reason is simple— men are not economic inputs. They are not replaceable automatons, each equally capable of a certain level of economic output. Economic theories that do not consider culture, history, tradition, and the biological reality of race simply do not work. Let it be said plainly—even in purely economic terms, socialism in Sweden beats capitalism in Haiti, every single time.

Once any foundational principle relinquishes the explicit identification of race, it contains the seeds of its own destruction. Rootless religion, abstract civic creeds, or arrogant economism devour themselves within generations, actively dispossessing their own constituencies. Collective suicide is hardly an endorsement of any of these theories.

In contrast, race, by itself, provides sufficient guidance. The upward development of the race must be the organizational principle of the state because it contains a non-negotiable core of continuity with the necessary tactical flexibility to respond to changing circumstances. It gives coherence to long-term state policy across a whole range of issues.

Take something as seemingly nonracial as transportation. Obviously, American transportation policy is hopelessly muddled because of the need to commute to avoid living in high crime black neighborhoods, the inability of non-whites to refrain from causing chaos and crime on public transportation systems, and the multicultural requirement to give government jobs to incompetent minorities, resulting in deadly accidents.[11]

However, in a White Republic, race could still guide policy even if we didn't have to deal with racial aliens. A folkish transportation policy would seek to integrate transportation within the framework of an organic society. It would work to reduce stress and conflict between members of the racial community. It would prioritize state investment to reduce costs for workers who need to get to their jobs, thus increasing overall economic productivity for the benefit of everyone. It would incorporate aesthetic, environmental, and even psychological concerns, so that something as mundane as getting from point A to point B wouldn't be a cause of tension and rage, but something that creates white communal unity. Of course, Golden Dawn in Greece took a small step in this direction by occupying privately owned toll booths, forcefully rejecting the idea that the nation's people are resources to be harvested for private benefit.

Race provides clarity. In health care, policies are intended to ensure quality of life and dignity for the racial community, rather than trying to ration care or protect the medical establishment. In population policy, the goal is to constantly improve the racial stock, creating healthier, more intelligent, more attractive people, creating a cascading series of benefits on a host of other issues. With family law, we break down the policies that set men against women and encourage legalistic arguments about property. Instead, we consciously pursue politics that enable strong, permanent, two-parent families that purposely set about to raise large numbers of legitimate children who are connected to their heritage and traditions. Instead of public policy guided by wishful thinking, irrele-

---

[11] http://www.washingtontimes.com/news/2012/mar/26/metro-derailed-by-culture-of-complacence-incompete/

vant tangents, or competing claims of imaginary rights, there is utter consistency.

The goal of any policy in any field is the survival and improvement of the *Volksgemeinschaft*—the organic racial community that transcends class. At different times and under different circumstances the policies may change, but the purpose remains.

Today, public policy discussion, especially on the Right, is characterized by a bizarre helplessness. On immigration, for example, even ideological conservatives with values above cheap labor seem resigned that their "principles" force them to approve their own dispossession. The North American New Right has to proclaim that any morality which mandates suicide, individual or collective, is to be destroyed. Morality exists to facilitate our development, not cripple us. Morality is a secondary development, a derivation, not a cause.

It is the upward development and survival that is the highest law, the law from which creeds, codes, and even gods must derive. Our people first—*Eigen Volk Eerst* as the Vlaams Belang says—is not just a populist political cry. It is a guide of policy, a framework of the state, the first moral commandment.

Counter-Currents/*North American New Right*,
May 14, 2013

WHAT MAKES REPUBLICANS TICK?

What exactly do they want?

You could understand if they were doing it for money. It's easy to maintain revolutionary integrity in the midst of poverty, but there are few who wouldn't be seduced by the promise of lifelong luxury and comfort. But they don't really get that.

You could understand if it was for social status. The fabled "cocktail parties" and pomp of the elite are even more tempting than a fat bank account. But they don't really get that either, and they are despised by the actual leaders of the culture.

You could understand if it was for power, or even the chance of power. Men will sacrifice almost anything for power, even family, love, or their most cherished ideals. But they don't get that. They never actually get what they want. If anything, they aren't even able to defend their own self-interest competently.

I understand the how. I don't understand the why.

What makes your average movement conservative tick?

The mystery of the American conservative movement is critical to understanding the barriers to White Nationalism in the United States. Regardless of whatever ideological absurdities, theological blasphemies, or simple intellectual cowardice plagues the American Right, the objective reality is that the American conservative movement is the most well-funded, active, and coordinated Right-of-Center movement in the Western world. Furthermore, regardless of the actual principles it espouses, the hard reality is that the American Right has increasingly become the political movement of American whites, and so there is bound to be overlap between the conservatives of the past and whatever movement arises to represent white Americans in the future.

I take as a premise that most people reading this book are already predisposed to scorn American conservatives. They are right—conservatives should be scorned. That said, they should not be underestimated.

The average activist or functionary in the Beltway conservative movement is competent, somewhat intelligent, focused, dedicated, and, of course, white. Let us be brutally clear—the average conservative is more capable of political activism than the average White Nationalist. More importantly, they can organize, fund, and perpetuate institutions that at least nominally move their cause forward, even as white advocates are forced to the fringe.

At the same time, conservatives never seem to actually get anywhere. The America of today, with its vast entitlements, massive government spending, and crumbling "Judeo-Christian" culture is much worse by their own standards even after the "Conservative Revolution" of Ronald Reagan and the Revolution of 1994. Some of the more farsighted among them, like Pat Buchanan and Mark Steyn, even know this explicitly. Nonetheless, the only thing they can think of to do is vote for a Mitt Romney, who shows no signs of halting the decay and may even accelerate it. Even the most incompetent and cartoonish White Nationalist who somehow converts one other person to the cause has accomplished more than all of these multimillion-dollar foundations put together. The quest for a white ethnostate at least has the theoretical potential for victory. Conservatism doesn't.

So why do they do it? Generally speaking, people join movements for one of three primary motivations: financial, ideological, or social. One of the most common criticisms of movement conservatives is that they are "in it for the money." It's true that many movement conservatives will actively restrain themselves from speaking certain truths or addressing certain topics for fear of losing their job. However, this isn't really the same thing as "selling out." Websites like Counter-Currents don't require commenters to post their names and phone numbers. Under the glorious democratic regime, normal people have to lie in order to protect their livelihood.

The truth is that conservatism as a profession doesn't pay very well. Sure, if someone is elected to Congress or runs a successful campaign, he might eventually make a great deal of money as a lobbyist or a consultant. However, most political activists lead terrible lives. The hours are long, the money is small or nonexistent, the food is terrible, and the influence is limited. You could run a brilliant campaign, only to lose at the last minute because of a gaffe or another person's mistake, and you are always the one who is expendable.

Jobs with nonprofits aren't much better, as they combine the work hours of a high-powered law firm with the average salary of a greeter at Walmart. Even for those who have the ambition, intelligence, drive, and luck to reach the heights, the salaries are nothing to those obtained by even young employees in investment banking or finance. To paraphrase what P. J. O'Rourke and many others have observed, the best minds on the Left go into politics while the best on the Right go into business. A conservative who pursues politics as a career for financial reasons is either absurdly confident, misinformed, or a complete idiot.

The second rationale, ideology, doesn't have much more to offer most conservatives. True, a small number of conservatives are willing to make sacrifices and work for their beliefs even when there is no reward. Take a young activist like James O'Keefe, who used video journalism to bring down ACORN and expose voter fraud by the son of a sitting Congressman (one of the few, it should be noted, critical of America's ties with Israel).

O'Keefe is occasionally hailed as a hero by the conservative Right, but is also condemned by them when his stunts don't quite work out. According to some reports, he is heavily in debt and fighting continuous legal battles[1]—but, mysteriously, all those rich conservative donors haven't helped him out even as he takes on such eminently kosher causes as proving that abortion providers are racist or that Democrats enjoy breaking election laws.

The vast majority of conservative activists seem to have a deep disquiet with actually seeking victory, with the possible exception of pro-lifers and libertarians. Pro-lifers are the one group of conservatives who are actually willing to be arrested for their cause. But the American pro-life movement holds to an even more radical egalitarian critique of American society than the liberals. White Nationalists have nothing to look for here.

Many of the grassroots libertarians are highly ideological and deeply dedicated. They have successfully developed a thriving subculture, complete with an internal economy. They operate both inside and outside of the system. They participate within the Republican Party and the conservative movement, but remain an independent force. They have their own overall *Weltanschauung* and institutions to meet activists at every level, from college students to serious academics.

Most of all, libertarians have a serious critique of the system, and they have something to say—as long as it doesn't get them in trouble with the wrong people. No matter how radical they are, most libertarians are cautious to apply their rigid beliefs only to those issues that fit with Left-wing talking points. If confronted by cultural Leftists, they will switch positions, run away, or active-

---

[1] http://www.huffingtonpost.com/2011/03/23/james-okeefe-credit-card-debt_n_839565.html

ly join the other side.[2] They may oppose the System, but like the pro-lifers, they oppose it because it is not egalitarian enough on issue like immigration, race, homosexuality, or national identity.

Conservative Christians of all denominations may believe they are acting out God's will on earth, but it is not a political version of holy war. Instead, the most militant evangelical Christians think God Himself will come down to sort out our affairs, and so our efforts will come to nothing. Insofar as they are passionately interested in the demographic situation of a nation, it is that of Israel, and a serious case can be made that evangelicals have evolved from worshiping a savior of Jewish blood to quite literally worshiping Jewish blood.

Many of the more hierarchical Christians such as Catholics or some of the Orthodox believe in their denominations, but in the bloodless modern way so as not to cause offense. Christianity is justified on the grounds that it led to modern liberalism. The actual tactics that were used to establish these churches go without defense. Insofar as there are movements seeking to reestablish Christian majorities, they are swiftly condemned.[3] It's telling that the legendary *National Review* columnist and fierce Catholic Joe Sobran was unceremoniously expelled from the movement for questioning Jewish domination, while anti-God crusader, enthusiastic blasphemer, and self-described man of the Left Christopher Hitchens was warmly welcomed even until his last days. While there might be the occasional joke about the Crusades or the Rapture, the God of the conservative

---

[2] http://www.vdare.com/articles/lew-rockwell-and-the-strange-death-or-at-least-suspended-animation-of-paleolibertarianism

[3] http://www.theamericanconservative.com/dreher/shame-on-greek-orthodox-nazis/

Christians is either an invisible Republican Martin Luther King Jr. who lives in the sky, a Pope issuing a bull on the need for more democratic elections, or an Israeli Prime Minister.

Russell Kirk, the brilliant reactionary author of *The Conservative Mind*, famously defined conservatism as "the negation of ideology." Instead, conservatism theoretically was an intellectual temperament with a mild partisan fixation. However, as "conservatism" became "Conservatism Inc.," conservatism simply became a word, a party line imposed by a series of interlocking institutions from the top down, designed to create talking points to elect preferred candidates.[4]

Insofar as there is an intellectual justification for conservatism, it accepts the American Founding as part of a gradual progression towards egalitarianism after the so-called Enlightenment.[5] The idea that the Enlightenment itself was problematic is outside the consensus. Conservatives see their mission as defending the existing system, with their dissent simply functioning as a way to make it more efficient. The difference between the American Right and Left seems to be that the former is willing to dragoon pre-modern institutions to better defend modernity, whereas the latter wants to extirpate traces of the traditional West altogether.

As Jonah Goldberg of *National Review* and *Liberal Fascism* writes:

[W]hatever our differences with American liberals may be, conservatives understand that our argument with them is still within the family. The fighting is intense, but we're all trying to figure out

---

[4] http://www.theamericanconservative.com/how-conservatism-lost-its-mind/

[5] http://takimag.com/article/americas_wise_latina_lady/

what it means to live in this country bequeathed to us by the American Revolution and the Enlightenment."[6]

It should be noted that for Goldberg, even Buchananism was too fascistic, because it hinted at a vision of an organic society.

American conservatism can't win because it is enlisted in the defense of a System openly hostile to the traditional loyalties of its followers. Regardless of how degenerate, egalitarian, and fundamentally Leftist American society becomes, conservatism will shift to interpret it as the new normal.[7] American conservatives lack a core coherent ideology to motivate them and somehow, at the same time, they deny the concrete realities of race, place, religion, and real nationhood in the name of an abstract proposition nation. It is the worst of all possible political movements. At a core level, it's not just that conservatives don't want to win—they don't even know what victory would mean.

This leaves the final factor as the real secret of conservative identity—the social factor. As with all movements, the conservative movement provides its participants with being part of a shared experience, a common subculture, and a social network of friends and colleagues. This alone has a great deal of seductive power. Once a person joins the conservative movement, for whatever reason, he will be hesitant to do anything which will lead to expulsion from respectable gatherings. This has less to do with honest fear of the Left than it does with losing the respect of conservative colleagues.

While this is a necessary part of the explanation, it's

---

[6] http://www.nationalreview.com/articles/328731/tribe-liberty-jonah-goldberg

[7] http://www.amnation.com/vfr/archives/023637.html

not sufficient. Modern conservatism, if it lacks a core system of beliefs, does contain certain vague feelings that are universally shared throughout the American Right. Chief among them is a sense of superiority among conservatives. This does not contradict the egalitarian ideology anymore than status-seeking SWPLs indulging in expensive sandwiches believe anything is awry with their behavior. Status seeking is universal among humans. It simply functions in perverted ways in ostensibly egalitarian societies.

Among Republicans, the devotion to capitalism and limited government operates not just as an economic platform, but as a social outlook. Even though the movement has manifestly failed to limit government in any substantive way, the insistence on seeing America as a meritocratic society gives Republicans a way to associate themselves with the successful. The fetishizing of "job creators," Mitt Romney's dismissal of the "47%," and the vulgar, simplistic interpretation of Ayn Rand as the prophet of the capitalistic superman reflect this self-image.

The problem, of course, is that Republican functionaries don't function in the business world. Teenagers with business cards, college students drinking scotch, and hacks making 20K a year wearing three-piece suits to the bar are an attempt to substitute the illusion of wealth and power for the thing itself. At the core of the Republican identity is the idea that "we still run this thing." The liberal rage against the rich and the privileged actually feeds Republican glee. As long as they do not jeopardize their position, liberal hatred helps bind conservatives together and distinguishes the elite from the rabble. Even in Obama's America, conservatives are forever the landed elites, pitying the vulgar mobs below.

Thus, conservatives accept the institutionalization of every new Left-wing victory. While they may complain about voter fraud, judicial activism, or mass immigration, the idea of championing a restricted franchise, nullifying laws, or recognizing identity based on ethnicity and culture is obviously unthinkable. After all, conservatives believe it's their system.

Working hard and engaging in revolutionary political action implies that you don't already control everything. As Saul Alinsky observed, one's concern with the ethics of means and ends varies inversely with one's personal interest in the issue, and one's distance from the scene of conflict. By considering themselves "above" smashmouth politics because of the illusion of control, Republicans can avoid getting their hands dirty. The more pessimistic can console themselves that the world will not see their like again but still maintain the casual air of the upper class. To be a Republican is to simultaneously believe that the country is going to hell but that it is the greatest country that ever existed, and somehow, we will always be in charge.

It's not that many Republicans aren't politically incorrect behind closed doors—after all, even the castrati of the College Republicans were singing "Stomping Out the Reds" not long ago.[8] It's that being controversial implies that you have to get your hands dirty, rather than having an air of amused mastery towards your political opponents.

Thus, White Nationalists who look to conservatives as possible allies are sure to be disappointed. They will fight even more fanatically than Leftists to protect their American illusions. After all, most conservatives think revolution is by its very nature Left-wing. It's therefore not surprising, but entirely logical, that Glenn Beck is opposed to Leftists because they could potentially lead to "Nazis

---

[8] http://www.tinyrevolution.com/mt/archives/000517.html

like the Golden Dawn in Greece."[9]

Being a conservative Republican involves a very specific kind of self-glorification. The premises of the Left (democracy, equality, anti-racism) aren't systemically challenged, but Republican activists believe they still control the System. The rhetoric about individualism, capitalism, and meritocracy provide a justification to ignore "collectivist" appeals to race and nation while glorifying the self. A revealing episode at the Conservative Political Action Conference involved the author discussing the British National Party with a group of American GOP and British Conservative activists. They were horrified by the BNP, not because the party was racist, but because it "supports the working class."

It should be noted that many conservatives really do believe that everyone can succeed if they "work hard," like the educator who claims that he won't stop until every student in the country is "above average." For example, even as Jesse Jackson Jr. stumbles through rehab, his Republican opponent (being crushed in the polls) says his primary goal is to have everyone move into the 1%, presumably starting with black urban dwellers.[10] Of course, if one accepts this premise, it means that Republicans who associate themselves with success get to glorify themselves even more, as they "earned it."

Less hypocritically than urban hipsters, conservatives have developed a way to show they are better than everyone else without actually having to adopt a systematic defense of hierarchy. Those nationalist appeals that are accepted are couched in rhetoric about democracy, equality, and "freedom." An appeal in the name of racial loyalty, traditional identity, or collective action can be

---

9 http://www.glennbeck.com/2012/10/01/is-the-golden-dawn-party-spreading-to-the-united-states/

10 http://www.woodworthforcongress.com/issues

safely ignored as all of these efforts imply subordination to a greater collective good.

The Right's fixation on American Exceptionalism is another exercise in self-deception, as the impulse for self-glorification is used to fuel chest-beating pride that America can defeat fascists and theocrats in the name of global democracy. In the end, Americanism itself becomes the real religion.

Even if the Left totally controls the country, they can still never be comfortable with any kind of patriotism. Regardless of how far the Long March proceeds in the United States, Leftists know the United States of America was built by and for the white race. The Right remains deliberately ignorant of historical realities, simply pretending that race doesn't exist and that there were black Founding Fathers. It's arguably more dangerous because it twists the natural impulses of patriotism, loyalty, and the striving for greatness into an ever-more irrational and conspiratorial ideology ever-more remote from what was good about this country.

To be a Republican offers the appearance of status, power, and responsibility without the reality. Like an unemployed black puffed up with pride because "our people" run his city of Detroit, Republican activists are a giant cargo cult of primitives who put the symbols of status before status itself. As the real America retreats from the immigration-inundated coasts, the culture collapses even in the Heartland, and the people demand an ever-greater welfare state, the Republican Party will continue to pretend they are defending their America.

Even Pat Buchanan, who has written book after book proclaiming the "Death of the West," thinks Mitt Romney can save us.[11] As Garet Garrett wrote, "There are

---

[11] http://www.counter-currents.com/2012/10/white-lies-buchanans-endorsement-of-romney/

those who still think they are holding the pass against a revolution that may be coming up the road. But they are gazing in the wrong direction. The revolution is behind them. It went by in the Night of Depression, singing songs to freedom."[12] It's worth noting that Buchanan also endorsed George W. Bush in 2004 on the grounds that he would give us conservative justices and that he simply could not align himself with the Democratic "tribe."[13] George W. Bush gave us the conservative John Roberts, who then saved Obamacare.

The businessman who cuts the checks to his *alma mater* that pay Left-wing faculty, the Republican frat boy who glories in his status even as his house is abolished because it's not "inclusive," the faithful churchgoer who wants to defend "Christian America" as they build a mosque in Murfreesboro, the Beltway defense intellectual who plots to maintain the military superiority of Barack Hussein Obama's Praetorians and bomb those evil tsarist Russians—all share the belief that this is still their country, and that rest of us just live here. While College Republicans can fantasize that being in the GOP will help them bag Southern sorority girls, those girls are too busy sleeping with their black high school students, and there's nothing that the supposed "white power structure" can do about it.

It's tempting to say, "Power resides where men believe it does," but that's not entirely true. Power is concrete, not just an illusion, and sometimes the appearance of weakness is used to disguise the reality of the iron fist. The Left would have us believe that the United States of America is run by an ultra-conservative racist, sexist, patriarchal WASP ruling class that is constantly oppressing

---

[12] http://www.lewrockwell.com/orig5/garrett1.html

[13] http://www.theamericanconservative.com/articles/coming-home/

everyone. The American Right would have us believe that they are that class, but they are actually governing benevolently for the good of everyone. It's a farce, of course, but it meets the psychological needs of both groups. In the twisted status competition of a nominally egalitarian society, the grassroots activists of the Republican Party are one giant "Wooden Titan" so committed to their fantasy of power they don't even realize they have been dispossessed.[14] American conservatism is social proof masquerading as a political movement, and it won't end until we end it.

Counter-Currents/*North American New Right*,
November 2, 2012

---

[14] http://www.vqronline.org/articles/1937/summer/hoover-wooden-titan/

WHY ROMNEY MUST LOSE

Worse is not necessarily better.[1] Obama's re-election is a defeat for white advocates. A successful black President will restructure the entire country along anti-white lines. And despite all of this—Mitt Romney must lose.

White advocates should understand at the beginning how desperately weak our position really is. We do not have the numbers to appeal to either major political party on a national scale. White Nationalists are also incredibly divided when it comes to political action—the price of being independent thinkers against the egalitarian ideology of the regime. We are perhaps the one constituency in the entire country that a politician can safely dismiss and even openly insult, saying "I do not want your support."

Nonetheless, Gregory Hood's first rule of White Nationalism remains true: the farther away a figure is from White Nationalism, the more likely White Nationalists are to sense sympathy or even quiet agreement. If one is so inclined, you can craft a semi-plausible case about how Romney is secretly on "our" side or how Barack Obama is at least "more independent of Israel." That said, let's not kid ourselves that we have any real impact on this election or a potential secret friend in the Oval Office. As a community, we are too divided, too marginalized, and simply don't have the numbers. The only reason we should care about this election at all is because of the impact it will have on our own organizational efforts. The only question we need to ask is, "Is it good for white advocates?"

---

[1] Greg Johnson, "'Worse is Better,'" in *New Right vs. Old Right* (San Francisco: Counter-Currents, 2013).

Let's start with the idea that Obama's re-election is actually an unqualified good thing for White Nationalism.[2] It's certainly true that Obama's first term has been a bonanza for white racial awareness. Most observers conclude that "racism" is rising among American whites,[3] or more accurately, whites are becoming increasingly impatient with liberal excuses for black dysfunction.[4] The initial promise that Barack Obama would be a "post-racial" President that could unite the country has already collapsed in ruins. The Obama regime has created the rise of the implicitly white and tactically populist Tea Party Movement and fueled an increasing radicalization of American conservatives. It's tempting to simply say that we want this process to continue and that we should favor Obama's second term for tactical reasons. Worse is better, right?

However, there will be formidable costs. If Barack Obama is defeated, America's first black President will go down as a failure, and there will be riots and disorder that will accelerate the fraying of this failed experiment we call the United States. If he is re-elected, barring some completely unforeseen disaster, he will go down as the liberal Reagan, a successful President who killed Bin Laden, passed his signature health care law, and pulled the country out of recession.[5] Regardless of predictions that "the Collapse" is nigh, the economy is improving (albeit slowly), and there is no reason to doubt that this

---

[2] Greg Johnson, "The 2012 US Presidential Election," in *Confessions of a Reluctant Hater*, 2nd ed. (San Francisco: Counter-Currents, 2016).

[3] http://www.pressherald.com/news/nationworld/in-focus-racism-in-america_2012-10-28.html

[4] http://stuffblackpeopledontlike.blogspot.com/2012/11/what-romney-victory-means-white-people.html

[5] http://www.thedailybeast.com/newsweek/2012/09/23/andrew-sullivan-on-the-promise-of-obama-s-second-term.html

will continue in the short term. While Americans may find it difficult to adjust to the new normal of high unemployment, adjust they will, and Republicans will find it difficult to attack Obama's record unless the country relapses into an actual recession.

Make no mistake—this is a defeat for whites, and will be interpreted as such. Even more than in 2008, blacks will see this on tribalist grounds as a triumph over their enemies. It opens the door for Obama to be introduced into the pantheon of great American Presidents like FDR or Lincoln, and the controlled media will do its best to create a mythology that will put Kennedy's Camelot to shame. Psychologically, it will be sickening.

With these costs in mind, it would be more than justified for white advocates to compromise and vote Republican if there was even a chance to limit the damage. It's easy to imagine hypothetical scenarios in which a Republican victory could fuel a renewed push towards a populist Right. Even anti-white mainstream political parties can inadvertently legitimize new viewpoints and fuel new political movements. This was the case following Republican presidential victories in the 1980s, when Pat Buchanan commented that "the largest vacuum in American politics is to the right of Ronald Reagan."

One of the more divisive debates in the history of the white advocacy movement took place during the 1992 Republican primaries, which featured Pat Buchanan and David Duke as candidates. Representative Duke used the usual tactics of fringe candidates, trying to embarrass Buchanan into associating with him, leading to scenes where Pat Buchanan literally ran away so he wouldn't be caught in a photograph. Obviously, to those opposed to white genocide, Pat Buchanan was acting like a coward.

That doesn't matter. If Pat Buchanan had won the GOP nomination and the White House (without Perot running to screw over George H. W. Bush, he would have), it would have fueled a new surge in patriotic activism at a time when it could have made a difference. Buchananite officials would have taken key positions in the Party. Elected officials would be forced to attack free trade, immigration, and cultural Marxism out of party loyalty. Everyone would know what issues and impulses were behind his rise, and they would move to exploit them. Even though Buchanan's policies were preferable to George H. W. Bush's (or Bill Clinton's), the more important effect is that it would have fueled further movement to the right. He wasn't a safety valve—he was gasoline on a fire.

In contrast, what would Mitt Romney lead to? Even his supporters don't really know what Mitt Romney believes about critical issues. He has run an oddly defensive campaign for a challenger, seemingly pinning all of his hopes on the poor economy. He has offered no positive vision for what he would do as President and has managed to antagonize the very white working-class voters in the Midwest (the Reagan Democrats) that would propel him to an easy victory.

The one constant of Mitt Romney's political philosophy is the redistribution of wealth to the rich. His running mate's brilliant idea is cutting Medicare payments that disproportionately benefit elderly whites—the one welfare program whites really benefit from. At a time when there is a real opening to mobilize against the parasitical bankers that have ripped apart the Western world, the Republican Party is offering us a parody of a vulture capitalist.

A Romney victory would be catastrophic on several fronts. Putting the equivalent of the Monopoly guy in the White House would be a massive shot in the arm to the Occupy movement and other elements of the activist Left. Leftists have done an excellent job of policing themselves to ensure that street opposition to the banks is monopolized by activists firmly committed to Left-wing social causes, open borders, and anti-white animus. While this has limited their appeal, with a corporate stooge in the White House they will be able to frame themselves as the populist alternative to a corrupt system. The result would be a re-energized Left, from the halls of Congress on down to the lowest antifa.

Romney's policies, like those of George W. Bush, would actively punish and dispossess his own base. It's not clear that Romney actually is the "lesser evil." An emphasis on finance capital and an indifference to white workers would exacerbate the class divisions ripping apart American whites.

Romney's swift adoption of the Chamber of Commerce position for unlimited cheap labor suggests that restrictionist Republicans would once again face the threat of national suicide at the hands of their own party. A Republican House is likely to dig in its heels against Obama's plan to ram through amnesty. A President Romney would actually be more likely to win over Republican defectors to join with the Democrats to deliver the death blow to white America.

That said, let's be honest—even if Obama is still the President, amnesty may be a *fait accompli*. There may be enough Newt Gingrichs and Jeb Bushes this time around to join the Democratic push for dispossessing the historic American nation. Amnesty will be the final nail in the coffin for any Republican presidential aspirations. It is critical that there is a black face on this action and that it is interpreted in racial terms as an aggressive act against "racist" whites. If Republicans do it, it will be simply be seen as a strategic mistake.

The most commonly advanced argument is the most unconvincing. After the fiasco of Chief Justice John Roberts, it should be embarrassing to suggest that whites should vote for Republicans in order to get "good judges." While Republicans have to pick judges who carefully refrain from expressing themselves on anything and then read the tea leaves to hope they are conservative, Democrats casually nominate their "wise Latinas" and activists from the ACLU. Republican-nominated Justices like David Souter and Sandra Day O'Connor would carefully look for legal rationales to preserve programs like affirmative action, whereas Justices like Ginsburg and Sotomayor casually toss aside whatever stands in the way of their policy preferences. After a half century of catastrophic judicial activism starting with the Warren Court (Earl Warren being nominated by the Republican Dwight Eisenhower), we simply don't have time for these games anymore.

Despite the claims of an "elected dictatorship," the President does not have independent freedom of action on domestic policy. Foreign policy should be far more important in the choice of a President. Here, Romney is not even close to the lesser of two evils, but is far worse. A Romney Administration would mark the return of the neoconservatives who have learned nothing and forgotten nothing.

The Obama Administration has overseen the transformation of the Middle East from generally pro-American (or at least easily bribed) autocrats into democratically elected paladins of the Muslim Brotherhood. Amazingly, Romney manages to simultaneously criticize the Obama Administration for allowing this process to occur while also saying he's not moving fast enough. He condemns Egypt's conquest by the Muslim Brotherhood but thinks we need to "do more" in Syria to achieve the same result.

Romney has also been boasting of his fealty to the Jewish state. A Romney presidency would accomplish the neat trick of increasing radicalization in the Muslim world, antagonizing Islamic populations through rampant interventionism and servility to Tel Aviv, and blowing American lives and treasure in adventures that make the country less secure. Once again, Americans will be sent to die for people who hate them. Romney would scoop out the worst filth of the Obama and Bush foreign policies, combine them, and unleash it on the world.

The worst part is that a President Romney would co-opt the frustrated patriotism of Middle Americans into supporting these pointless quagmires. With President Obama, there is at least an opening to argue that foreign interventionism is actually targeted against Middle America. The current cold war between the Navy SEALs and the Obama Administration is a key division white advocates would be wise to exploit. We want to encourage the idea of a *Dolchstoß*, a stab in the back of brave patriots by a civilian leadership that despises them. It also happens to be true.

However, with President Romney, Middle Americans would support these interventions and unleash another wave of pointless false patriotism. Worst of all, the primary target of a Romney Presidency would be Russia, our number one geopolitical foe. In its dying gasps, the might of the American Empire would be marshaled to destroy what little white anti-system resistance remains against the global order of liberal capitalism. Much like under George W. Bush, the Left would be free to exploit popular anger against wasteful foreign wars. Instead of a populist uprising against an exploitative anti-white system, we would see a rising Left mobilizing against the racist, patriarchal Empire of white supremacist religious extremist Mitt Romney.

This is the heart of the issue. If white advocates are to triumph, we have to become the popular opposition to the ruling system. It's not just what policies are followed, it's about how they are interpreted. If Romney is President, it once again forces the white advocacy community into a reactionary stance, defending the corrupt American ruling class and its financial masters against an anti-white Left with renewed revolutionary *élan*. Unlike a President Pat Buchanan, Mitt Romney would generate no momentum to the revolutionary Right. Instead, he would gradually retreat, apologetically, embarrassingly, on all of the issues that are important to us. His only strong stands would be in defense of his old colleagues at institutions like Bain Capital.

Emotionally, of course I want Romney to win. Of course it will be sickening to watch the celebrations on MSNBC or in the college towns around the country. The aforementioned costs are real. However, we must remember that the United States of America has already been lost. We can no longer afford to read into things what we wish to exist, rather than what actually is there.

Worse is not always better, but in this case it is. We have no alternative to offer anyone at this time. Our enemy is this system. Therefore, our best bet is for this system to be revealed for what it is—a parasitical institution dedicated to destroying white communities and degrading the best in humanity for the benefit of exploitative plutocrats and twisted culture distorters. A friendly white face doesn't change anything.

Even if, under the most sympathetic reading, Mitt Romney does want to help, there is nothing in his career or life to suggest that he will actually do anything to actively oppose the Left-wing forces arrayed against him. When this system fails, we have to be sure it is identified with the right people and that the right people get the blame.

We have to delegitimize the regime, and most white people vote for the Republicans. Therefore, we want to encourage the idea President Obama's government is an occupier. This is already happening. Birtherism is the desperate attempt of conservatives to believe in constitutionalism and Americanism without having to draw racial conclusions. Soon, even this thin reed will be taken away. If Obama is re-elected after months of a triumphant victory narrative among Republicans, many will believe that the election was stolen. Reports of bused-in Somalis swinging the vote, corrupt political machines in major cities, and threats of black riots are all to the good. A situation in which Mitt Romney wins the popular vote but loses the electoral vote would be even better.

White Americans need to understand that they can't elect their way out of this crisis; that it is literally no longer possible. They need to understand that it is the System itself that is against them, and readings of the Constitution won't save them.

This doesn't mean Republicans are irrelevant. It doesn't mean third parties are irrelevant. It doesn't mean partisan democratic politics are irrelevant. They are all relevant insofar as they lead people to us. What it means is that we have to craft an independent force to save our race and advance our ideas and policies.

This election is not our fight. We have to engage in politics on our own terms. Even mainstreamers should dedicate their time and talents only to movements and figures that can lead to greater things, not sacrifice for people who will continuously retreat from the day they are elected.

No one else will do it. It will take everything we have to save ourselves. We shouldn't dedicate anything we have, even our votes, to saving our enemies.

Counter-Currents/*North American New Right*,
November 5, 2012

A White Nationalist Memo to White Male Republicans

Do you get it yet?

Look, I know you probably despise us. You've been told your entire life—by your schools, your churches, and your heroes of sport, stage, and screen—that there is no greater sin than racism. You wanted to be a good person. Heck, you are a good person.

So you treated everyone with respect, no matter where they came from. You figured everyone should have an opportunity. You believed in playing by the rules. You believed in freedom. You believed in America. You thought that what makes this country great is that everyone, from whatever background, can make it together. You may have even voted for Obama that first time, despite some policy disagreements, because you really wanted to believe that race is irrelevant, that skin tone doesn't matter, that the only colors we need are Red, White, and Blue.

You're a conservative, maybe even a libertarian. But you don't want to make "arbitrary" distinctions between people. After all, we're all children of our Creator. So you gave Obama a chance.

Unfortunately, instead of hope and change, you got a national health care program that frightened you and increased your health care costs. You got more racial division, not less. The economy didn't improve—in some places, it got worse. There was a huge stimulus program—but you can't say what all that money was spent on. And because you care about your country, you worry about the debt, and federal spending, and fiscal responsibility.

So you supported Mitt Romney. Perhaps you even

participated in a Tea Party rally or two a few years ago, careful to stick to fiscal issues rather than divisive social concerns. You were embarrassed by how white the rallies were and did your best to bring in racial minorities. You liked Herman Cain. You liked Allen West. You wanted to get blacks off the Democratic plantation.

The economy was collapsing so you supported a campaign focused on growing the pot for everyone. You said a rising tide lifts all boats. You talked about jobs, about growth, about making America proud again. You talked about how blacks are hit more than anyone else by the bad economy, how Hispanics in Nevada have been devastated by crushing unemployment, how a culture of dependency is taking root in entire communities. And you believed the conservative pundits that told you that America was rising, as one, to bring about real change.

And because you're a patriot, you felt justified in being angry. You felt your blood boil when you read how Americans begging for help as terrorists stormed into our embassy were contemptuously ignored for hours. Your heart broke when you read about the mother of the Navy SEAL crying out in anguish that "Obama murdered my son" and a grieving father at his son's funeral treated to our buffoon of a Vice President joking about testicles. Your jaw dropped when Bill Clinton gloated that the military is "less racist, less sexist, less homophobic" now that Barack is in charge. You watched in disbelief as the President of the United States palled around with interviewers on hip hop shows like the "Pimp with a Limp" on the anniversary of 9/11 and used former crack dealers turned rappers on the campaign. You knew something was wrong, but come Election Day, we'd "Remember in November," and America would be America again.

And then this.

So you're probably in a state of shock. They all lied to you. It wasn't even close. Ohio, Pennsylvania, even Virginia—Virginia!—the great Southern state of Washington, Jefferson, and Lee. All went to Barack Obama. And as you watched the gloating on MSNBC, the victory parties in the major cities, the undisguised loathing for you at the likes of *The Huffington Post*, or *Gawker*, or *Slate*, you had a sick feeling in your gut that something was deeply wrong.

Mitt Romney won the same share of the white vote as Ronald Reagan. It didn't matter. You worked your butt off with your church, your charity group, your neighbors. It was undone by some Somalis who can't speak English that the Democrats bused in and told to vote "Brown all the way down," and they weren't just referring to the Democratic candidate's name.

Take a good, hard look at those Obama victory rallies. They are celebrating your dispossession, your displacement from the country your ancestors built. They don't even disguise their hatred. And even though you don't think in terms of race, they do.

Michael Moore called it a victory over hate. Howard Fineman gloated that America was turning its back on tradition, and thank God. Twitter erupted with black voters screeching in triumph, bragging that America belongs to them now.

Even the President of the United States said "voting is the best revenge." Revenge for what? Aren't we all in this together? Doesn't this country belong to all of us?

Do you get it yet? It's revenge against *you*—for existing. It's revenge for "racism," for conservatism, for success, for being strong and proud and accomplished. It's vengeance against the America that once was. They have their revenge for the fact that your country existed. Barack Obama is President of these states united, and was re-elected *because*, not in spite of the fact that he despises everything America was.

Look, I was like you. I was a patriotic, normal Republican. I knocked on doors for city council. I wanted Colin Powell to be President, because "a black Republican will help everyone get beyond race!" I was there too.

And then I started looking around.

It doesn't matter if black unemployment is skyrocketing and their communities are devastated—they vote black. It doesn't matter if Nevada has the worst economy in the country—they vote Hispanic. It doesn't matter if candidates are running for re-election from the Mayo Clinic, or Congressmen think islands tip over if too many people are on them, or if blacks are worse off, by every measure, when African-Americans are in charge. It simply doesn't matter.

There are vast swaths of the country where elections, policies, and good government simply no longer matter. Camden, NJ, Detroit, MI, Birmingham, AL, and other once proud metropolises are shattered wastelands, and they are lost—forever—regardless of how bad they get. Let's make it perfectly clear—George W. Bush was probably the last Republican President this country will ever see. Once you go black, your country doesn't come back.

Perhaps you think it will all be OK if the GOP just wins the Hispanic vote. After all, Newt Gingrich and Karl Rove tell you they are socially conservative and patriotic. Unfortunately, they favor Obamacare even more than they favor unrestricted immigration. They have their problems with President Obama—because he doesn't support immigration enough. If you want to win the minority vote, you have to become more liberal on economic issues. Even the Beltway conservatives know it. And despite what your ministers and priests tell you about "Christian Hispanics," they have higher rates of illegitimate births and abortions too.

Well, *c'est la vie*. America is still America. Government isn't everything right? You can still have a decent life in this country, right?

Right?

You probably have a kid or two. Do you have any illusions about what he is learning in school? He is being taught that white people are uniquely evil, that he is the recipient of unearned "privilege" because he was born, and that to be a moral person, he has to turn his back on his ancestors—i.e., you. If you're a Christian, you're faithfully taking your child to church once a week—and five days a week he's being taught about the glories of homosexuality, or the wonders of Islam, or how black people single-handedly built Western civilization. None of it makes sense—except that it is all targeted against you.

Let's say you send him to college. Well, he can look forward to paying off student loan debt for the rest of his life. It would be great if he could get free money for college on account of his race, but he's white, so no one cares about him. This assumes your child can even get into a decent school, as every major school in the country fiercely defends anti-white racial preferences.

What will he learn there? Well, he will be carefully taught to despise you, that your religion is nonsense, and that his heritage is evil. Professors admit this is their job. But the fiscal crunch will cut the fat, right? Actually, schools are cutting mathematics and serious programs, while shoveling more money to anti-white programs. The school will pay tens of thousands of dollars of your tuition money to bring in guys like Tim Wise, who will gloat that "CONSERVATIVE WHITE PEOPLE, yr nation has left the building." And all these professors, and anti-racist guest lecturers, and professional "activists" for causes you've never heard of will make more money than you ever will—and you're paying their salaries.

Now that you've bankrupted yourself and burdened your child with student loans, it's time for him to get a job. Unfortunately, there are few to be had. The government is still hiring, but unfortunately your "white privilege" doesn't extend to having a job.

You know who else defends anti-white racial preferences? Corporate America. The 1% is actually pushing for diversity even more than the universities. Walmart, McDonald's, Microsoft, and all the great "job producers" that you've been defending? They despise you, give money to your enemies, and discriminate against you because you're white. When your right to be treated equally went before the Supreme Court, sixty-eight Fortune 500 companies filed amicus briefs to make sure you and your children can't get jobs. Those are the people you want to give tax cuts.

Want to have a small business? Better not try to do anything with the government or with federal funds—those are set aside for minorities. Also, any of your non-white competitors get special financial benefits for operating, so good luck competing. Incidentally, Barack Obama is going to dump some more regulations and taxes on you, especially through Obamacare. The Secretary of the Treasury doesn't have to pay taxes, but, well, you do.

Well, maybe you want to be a cop or a fireman then. You can't. Those jobs are set aside for minorities, even those who can't pass the test. Especially those who can't pass the test. Remember those heroic NYC firefighters on 9/11? Well, your government sued them for being too white and racist. Even dying for your masters doesn't get you anything.

Let's say, against all odds, you manage to get a job. Well, better keep your head down. You never know when a co-worker will accuse you of racism or sexism. There doesn't need to be a reason—it could just be out of spite. Or because you're Republican. Or because you reported them for stealing or incompetence. If anything, count yourself lucky they don't shoot you—the media will report that you, as a racist, had it coming. Every moment of every day, you are on the brink of professional and personal destruction, because you are white.

At least you can come home to a loving family right? Well, if your children watch television, they are being carefully instructed to disregard anything you teach them. Even children's programming executives laugh about how what they do is a "fuck you to the right wing." When they grow up, they'll worship celebrities of dubious talent who mock and despise you. You're surrounded by filth—you can't go to a restaurant or a store without background music from some bimbo relying on autotune to "sing" about S&M or threesomes.

Of course, that's assuming your kids aren't another victim of "random" crime by "youths."

As a father, sitcoms portray you as an idiot. As a husband, commercials mock you as sexually undesirable because of your race. As a white man, movies openly call for you to be killed. And if by chance you do something admirable, why, Hollywood simply changes your race.

And what about your wife? Of course you love her. But what is the culture telling her? If she leaves you, she gets your kids, your money, and any future earnings. The culture tells her she has no obligation to you or your children. The law rewards her if she abandons you. The media tells you the real problem is a "war on women." Maybe you've got a great girl, but just take a glance around the broken families and shattered men around this country, and ask yourself if the United States is a fit place for decent men and decent families.

Starting to get it yet? Every moment of every day, you have to bend the knee. Then, maybe, they'll let you have your job so you can pay taxes to sustain people who hate you. Maybe you'll have the privilege of working long hours to pay the mortgage, which costs you more because you're white. Maybe you can spend a few years with the children that the entire society is trying to turn against you. Maybe you can have a dinner with the woman you love and hope that she can ignore the culture telling her she's a traitor to her sex by staying with you. Maybe you can avoid the doom that hangs over your head every second.

And then, you can die. In fact, hurry up and do it. The Democrats are becoming bolder in just telling you these things.

The worst part is you'll have it easy compared to your kids.

Then, when it's all over, your life wasn't nothing. It was less than nothing. You actively contributed to your own destruction. Despite your surrender and respectability, you'll be remembered as a racist, a relic of an evil society.

Want to change this? Well, you will never have the possibility of Republicans fixing the problem for you. Ever again.

This isn't *Network*. I'm not going to tell you I don't know how to make things better. I'm not going to tell you to get angry. I know you're angry, and it hasn't done a damn bit of good for you or anyone else.

I'm going tell you what the solution is.

Everything you loved about what used to be your country came from one group of people. It's the group you belong to. It's the white race. And it's not an accident that the same people who hate your country, your religion, and your family hate your race more than anything.

You're a white man. "American" doesn't mean anything anymore. If anything, citizenship is actually a burden. As a white American, you are a second-class citizen in jobs, education, and government benefits. No one cares about you, and no one ever will. Those in power will deny that your suffering even exists. So why are you fighting for these people?

The nation you loved is still there. But it's not in the flag of a government that hates you or in the guns that serve people who don't care about you. It's in the faces of the white people that built this country and that sustain it today. That's what you have to fight for.

You need to fight for a country of your own. We need revolution if ordinary people anytime, anywhere are to have anything even close to a decent and happy life. And it makes more sense than spending your rapidly diminishing days shuffling through this horrifying nightmare that used to be your country.

You aren't alone. We're fighting for it right now. I can't force you to join us. I don't know where you are in your life.

But I want you to know one thing. You can't pretend you don't know anymore.

You can't kid around with talk about "taking back the country," or "freedom," or "liberty," or the "Real America." This is the Real America now. This is freedom. This is what it led to. This is the only thing it could have led to. What happened to the American Dream? It came true. "Equality" is being taken to its logical conclusion— and all you can ever hope for is serving the people who hate you.

You can't pretend this is still your country or that you are a free man. You aren't.

You can't pretend that you can keep playing by the rules and somehow win. You won't.

I'm not saying you need to drop everything. I'm not pretending I know exactly what to do. But I'm saying you need to remind yourself each morning that you are a slave, and people who hate you rule you. I'm saying you need to recognize that America today is a filthy lie, the most vile and despicable fiction ever foisted upon decent people. I'm saying everything good and generous about you is being used to kill you. I'm saying there are people out there like us who really care about you and want to help you. Your government and your society do not.

You can ignore me. Wave the American flag and pretend everything is going to be OK. But it won't be. Turn on the TV. Listen to the radio. Look—*really look*—at the culture that surrounds you. I think you know it too.

Do you get it yet? America, your America, is finished. But you don't have to be. It's time to fight for what comes next. It's time to fight for a country of our own.

It's time to stop being Americans. It's time to start being White Men again.

Counter-Currents/*North American New Right*,
November 9, 2012

How to Destroy the Republican Party

White advocates have no political power. White advocates have all the political power.

Those who don't favor the genocide of the white race have been completely marginalized. And yet, in another sense, White Nationalists dominate American life.

To paraphrase Marx, where is the party in opposition that has not been decried as "racist" by the party in power? Where is the opposition party that has not cleverly retorted that their enemies are the "*real* racists"?

Sometimes it seems that American political debate boils down to accusing the other side of being like those evil White Nationalists. This suggests that the world recognizes that White Nationalism is "itself a power," a power that cannot be ignored. You can love us or hate us, but you can't pretend we don't exist. Underlying every issue that is debated—guns, health care, immigration, foreign policy—is the reality of *race*, the undercurrent that is never spoken about by the Right but that dominates American life.

Much of white advocates' political activity, other than pure education, consists of trying to bring this undercurrent to the surface. Unfortunately, White Nationalist political influence within the mainstream is chiefly negative. Associating with certain groups or figures hurts their credibility with the larger public, which is conditioned by the controlled media to remain anti-white.

However, there is a positive side to this. We aren't here to elect Republicans after all. If activists concentrate enough on a certain subculture or political issue, it becomes associated with the white advocacy movement. Those hostile to white survival avoid it, but it can still serve as a way to attract unattached people who might be interested. Subcultures like folkish heathenism or black metal are cultural examples, and Southern nationalism is moving this way as a political example.

One can imagine issues like immigration or guns evolving in a White Nationalist direction. As groups that focus on such issues become racialized, many people will bail out, but those who remain involved will become more dedicated, and a "safe space" will be carved out for white advocates to organize. Furthermore, these spaces will still exist even if they are no longer respectable. This is why Leftists fight so hard to prevent white advocates from participating in even non-political venues, especially music scenes.

"The power to destroy a thing is the power to control a thing," said Paul Muad'Dib in *Dune*. Believe it or not, White Nationalists have this power. Take the conservative movement. All it takes to demolish a conservative gathering is for *one* person to show up with a "racist" sign. There are costs to such actions, obviously. In the short term, it makes it more difficult for any white advocates who are trying to work within the movement. It increases the internal defenses of the anti-white thought police within conservatism. It empowers a progressive media, which gleefully trumpets any proof of racism.

However, in the long term, *it creates an association in the public mind between a major political force and the cause of white people generally*. Isn't that what we want?

James Mason writes in *Siege* that white advocates must think of all white people everywhere as our army. They may not volunteer, but circumstances and political action will cause them to be conscripted. For white advocates, the overall strategic objective of political activity is to *make race the defining difference* between various political, cultural, and social groups, as a precursor to the formation of an ethnostate, the great dream of the White Republic.

Arguably, race is already the defining difference on a host of issues, but only on a subconscious level. The explicit issues are things like "limited government," capitalism vs. socialism, or religion vs. secularism. We have to cut through the distractions and bring out what is already implicit in the narratives we see every day.

How do we do this?

Do we just show up where we are not wanted, screwing up mainstream conservative plans?

It's a start. But this can't just be trolling.

A successful movement has to have waystations that we control all along the political spectrum. Part of this means overt vanguardist groups for the true believers. But another part of it means creating cultural spaces: publishers, websites, bands, or spiritual groups. Yet another part of it means trying to reclaim turf from the Left, like unions or the environment.

However, for now, the bulk of White Nationalists' power consists in the power to destroy.

If our goal is to make all white people our "army," we have to deal with the fact that the largest group of politically active whites is affiliated with the Republican Party.

One of the perennial debates in White Nationalism is between attacking conservatives, working with them (or infiltrating them), or just ignoring them. The correct answer is essentially "all of the above."

Everyone knows that there are certain issues—immigration being the key example—that come as close as they can to being defined as purely "racial" without crossing the line. The media knows this, non-whites know this, and white advocates know this. The only people who don't already know this are the professional anti-immigration groups and activists, and this ignorance (deliberate or otherwise) is the thin reed that allows them to continue to operate and have a voice at the system's table.

There's no point in showing up to an anti-immigration rally talking about a non-white America. *Everyone* involved in the issue already knows that this is what it is about, and the battle lines are already drawn. All overt White Nationalist participation in the issue can do is make their job harder, lessen the numbers of un-committed people who want to engage in the issue, and reduce the value of the movement as a whole. It is better to show up quietly, make new contacts, and educate and move them along separately and below the surface to waypoints further along the spectrum.

In contrast, something broad, like the general opposition to President Barack Hussein Obama, *should* be ra-cialized. The two-party system leads to political group-ings that are so broad that ideology is less important than emotional identification. "Team Red" vs. "Team Blue" means more than ideology. So forget the idea that the Republican Party is "anti-white," because there is no monolithic party the same way there is in Europe. Any-one can call himself a Republican. The broader, more inclusive, and more race-neutral a Republican group is, the riper it is for infiltration.

The media are looking for signs that the Republican Party is transforming into an all-white, rump opposition party that opposes the President purely on racial grounds. White advocates should give them what they want. The case that should be made is essentially the Mantra: the system is anti-white.

A single sign at a Tea Party rally that says "Obama is Anti-White" will make every blog. A post on the Cam-paign for Liberty website that "the government targets whites" will go viral. Showing up to an Americans for Prosperity meeting to ask a question about why non-white small business owners get special advantages, which "hurts whites," will become the subject of every discussion afterward.

The key is to *racialize* every mainstream issue, to make implicit racial polarization *explicit*. Constantly emphasize that (1) the government is targeting whites on racial grounds and (2) the opposition is organized on racial lines. The media will do the rest of the work, since they will promote anything that fits their own narrative of angry white males standing in the way of progress. So much the better.

George Lincoln Rockwell often spoke about "political jujitsu," using the very power of the controlled media to his advantage. Rockwell accomplished this with outrageous stunts and imagery that could not be ignored, especially that of the swastika. Today, the media's hysteria over "racism" has advanced to the point where such tactics are no longer necessary to get attention. Something as harmless as a Confederate flag at a war memorial or a white student union can throw the whole country into an artificially produced uproar. This is an opportunity to exercise power, because the media can do white advocates' job for them.

Media people think that tax protesters are racist. Good. Argue that whites are hit with a "disproportionate impact" in any tax increase and that this is deliberately discriminatory.

Media people think that gun owners are racist. Good. Argue that whites disproportionately own guns because non-whites disproportionately commit crimes.

Media people think states' rights are racist. Good. The best way to further this is to argue that Barack Obama's "drive for equality" is about using federal power to target whites.

In every case, make the point that the egalitarian principles of the system are violated when it comes to whites. Make race the central question even on issues that were once considered race-neutral.

The media will broadcast these reasonable positions

in tones of shock and outrage, but they will broadcast them nonetheless, and the effect is bound to be educational.

- ❖ Some of our people will begin thinking racially.
- ❖ They will see that the system is stacked against us.
- ❖ They will also know that there are people out there who will represent their racial interests.
- ❖ And they will see mainstream Republicans rushing to denounce and silence them.

We want to *increase* media criticism of Obama's opponents as racists. We want to *increase* the feeling that minority conservatives are Uncle Toms and race traitors for hire (which they largely are). We want to *increase* the reliance of the Republican Party on white voters, so it is harder and harder for them to ignore or betray white interests.

In our own consciousness, we need to consider ourselves *already* the true leaders and authentic spokesmen of our race, and we need to communicate that attitude to everyone else.

It's important to clarify that this is simply a tactic. It's a separate question if the Republican Party can be reforged into a pro-white party or used for anything practical. Nor should this strategy actually concede egalitarianism as a desirable goal. The point is to use the Left-wing media to sow discord in the controlled opposition and break some people away from it.

We should also do the same thing to the libertarians.

Simply criticizing Republicans from the outside is useful, but it is not enough, because it largely goes unheard. Race-based criticism from within, amplified by the media's bias against the Establishment Right, can destroy the controlled opposition and open the way for a new alternative. A well-written article on Counter-Currents can be read by tens of thousands. A well-staged stunt at a Republican event can be seen by tens of millions.

We have power. We have the sexiest idea there is. We know this because they can't shut up about us. Let's use it. Whites will become our army when we force everything down to a simple choice: The System is anti-white. We are pro-white. Which side are you on?

Counter-Currents/*North American New Right*,
January 31, 2013

WHY CHRISTIANITY CAN'T SAVE US

The conservative philosopher Russell Kirk wrote:

> We must remind ourselves, to begin, that culture arises from the cult: out of the religious bond and the sense of the sacred grow any civilization's agriculture, its common defense, its orderly towns, its ingenious architecture, its literature, its music, its visual arts, its law, its political structure, its educational apparatus, and its mores. Christopher Dawson, Eric Voegelin, and other historians of this century have made this historical truth clear.[1]

Kirk believed that Western civilization could not survive apart from an active and vigorous Christianity. Like many of the more traditionalist elements of the American Right, Kirk was a convert to Roman Catholicism. However, ultimately Kirk's traditionalism was pushed aside within American conservatism as the ideological premises of radical individualism, egalitarianism, and free market fundamentalism were taken to their logical conclusion. Furthermore, as American conservatism is essentially one giant corporate lobbying effort, the coherence of an ideology was less important than the interests of donors, and there are few donors who want to fund a kind of Christian traditionalism.

More importantly, Christianity itself is complicit in the "leveling" process. As Alain de Benoist has described in *On Being a Pagan*,[2] creation in the Christian conception is an

---

[1] http://www.touchstonemag.com/archives/article.php?id=06-01-005-f

[2] Alain de Benoist, *On Being a Pagan*, ed. Greg Johnson, trans. Jon Graham (Atlanta: Ultra, 2004).

alienating process, as consciousness and the divine is held to be outside a fallen world. As Benoist argues, Christianity and monotheism generally pave the way for atheism by desacralizing the world. The result is plagued with a hatred for the world as it is, a world-denying impulse that naturally lends itself to messianic liberalism to make the fallen world fit with the divine order. Eric Voegelin termed this attempt to bring heaven to Earth as the impulse to "immanentize the eschaton."

And of course, that divine order is, at its heart, egalitarian. Though Christianity properly understood does not demand egalitarianism, racial suicide, or messianic liberalism, the central doctrines of the cult of the cross make this evolution natural. Like acid, Christianity burns through ties of kinship and blood. As Christ states, "He that loves father or mother more than me is not worthy of me: and he that loves son or daughter more than me is not worthy of me" (Matthew 10:37). The Apostle Paul tells us, "There is neither Jew nor Greek, there is neither bond nor free, there is neither male nor female: for ye are all one in Christ Jesus" (Galatians 3:28).

While he understandably downplays the Jewish role in cultural breakdown, Paul Gottfried's *Multiculturalism and the Politics of Guilt: Toward a Secular Theocracy* effectively makes the case that residual Protestantism is part of the ideological justification for "equality," as the redeemed seek to display their elect status through superior displays of liberal morality.[3] Though God Himself has been deposed for being too inegalitarian, the old Yankee spirit of messianic egalitarianism persists to the present day within secular, post-Protestant America.[4]

---

[3] Paul Gottfried, *Multiculturalism and the Politics of Guilt: Toward a Secular Theocracy* (Columbia: University of Missouri Press, 2002).

[4] http://www.vdare.com/posts/opening-borders-as-the-

Of course, this still leaves the more traditionalist churches such as the Roman Catholic, the Orthodox, and the remnants of traditional Protestantism. Many of these denominations are growing as the moribund institutions of mainline Protestantism continue to wither away. However, the hierarchies, rituals, and doctrines that sustain these denominations owe more to ethnic traditions, political realities, or nods to Primordial Tradition than anything within Christianity itself. As James Russell exhaustively documented in *The Germanization of Early Medieval Christianity*, what we think of as orthodox (small "o") Christianity in the West is a cultural conglomeration of ostensible Christian belief forced into the world-accepting, hierarchical, and warrior societies of the Germanic West. Even today, the same Christian leader who tours Third World slums bemoaning inequality bears the title of the Roman guardian of the state religion (Pontifex Maximus). The warrior saints like St. Michael and St. George, the character of the High Mass, the cult of Mary, the sacralizing of political power or special objects—all of this owes more to paganism than any kind of authentic Christian belief.

Militant Protestantism would confirm these exact same charges. For hundreds of years, the Christian cross itself was not a sacred symbol to devout Christians, but an offensive reminder of Roman "paganism." In the 1965 film *Cromwell*, the eponymous hero interrupts a service to destroy a simple display of a cross and candles, thundering, "Would the king turn the house of God into a Roman temple?" Once Christianity is reduced to what it really is, it loses much of its role as a guardian of Tradition, a steward of the folk, or a positive force in the development of the race.

For any who accept "justification by faith," salvation or

damnation is conferred by an abstract individual choice as to whether or not one accepts Jesus Christ as the savior. Such a creed renders family, kin, and nation irrelevant, and it encourages intellectual stagnation so as not to endanger the soul of the believer. The most Bible-believing Christians, modern evangelical Protestants, are gradually transforming Christianity into its true form, a cult of egalitarian true believers, with the special "Chosen People" serving as the sole exception.

The contradiction at the heart of this process is that Christians remain the most Traditionalist mass constituency in the United States today, generally holding to conservative gender norms, having large families, and insisting on standards of decorum and hierarchy in behavior. Still, this can be explained because Christians are drawing on the cultural norms and standards of residual Westernized, "Germanized" Christianity. Even this is fading with time.

The influential evangelical preacher Rob Bell made headlines with his declaration that "Love Wins," suggesting that the Biblical ideal of hell needs to be rethought. Younger evangelicals are more likely to focus on issues of "injustice," poverty, and anti-racism rather than holding the line on issues like homosexual marriage. Even the pro-life cause has been justified by a kind of consistent and radical egalitarianism, rather than support of the traditional patriarchal family as such.

In *Men–Art–War,* a disillusioned priest says, "Where the Papists had made man a corpse, the Protestants had taken that corpse and made it a skeleton. From dead to deader, you could say."[5] Christianity is fatally handicapped by its insistence that people rationally believe irrational creeds, and the more they believe them, the more rem-

---

[5] Mikulas Kolya, *Men–Art–War* (Lincoln, Nebraska: iUniverse, 2006), p. 66.

nants of Tradition, culture, and life present within a denomination are stripped away. Traditional Catholicism (which is to say, a mixture of European paganism and mutilated Christian belief) simply decreed dogmas and told people to believe them. Protestants try to argue people into belief, which is why a modern evangelical sermon resembles nothing so much as a lawyer making a closing argument, using Scripture as his law.

Orthodoxy avoids some of the traps by emphasizing the mystical nature of God and his ultimately unknowable essence while retaining a strong hierarchical structure linked to culture and community in this world. It is not surprising that Orthodoxy has been gaining strength, especially in conservative circles, and that Orthodoxy alone does not seem to be explicitly committed to the extermination of white racial identity. It's also not surprising that the Culture Distorters have targeted Orthodoxy specifically as an obstacle to progress.

Of course, as a friend put it after watching an Orthodox nationalist rally, "Impressive, but eventually they are going to start reading their Bibles." By removing the protective shield of an esoteric priesthood around Christian doctrines, the Enlightenment, literacy, technology, and the Protestant revolution made Christian belief widely accessible to the masses. The result is that stripped of superstition and dogma, Christianity is being taken to its logical conclusion. The specific beliefs of Christian denominations are less important than their universalist message of salvation and overall moral and metaphysical outlook.

The acceptance of homosexuality and the removal of Christian symbols from the public square should not disguise the fact that the modern world is becoming *more* Christian.[6] Its universalism, its rejection of "unchosen"

---

[6] http://altright-archive.net/main/blogs/untimely-

loyalties of kin and country, its egalitarianism, its insistence on "human rights," and its embrace of a non-judgmental Savior make it a harmless spiritual outlet for the modern world, a way for those who can't fully grasp secular humanism to let off a little steam. Only Christianity's insistence that Jesus is in fact Lord separates it from being fully assimilated into modernity, and even this is being compromised.

Christianity was the essential religious step in paving the way for decadent modernity and its toxic creeds. In fact, many of the faith's leading spokespeople defend it for this reason—begging to be allowed to exist because it paved the way for "democracy" and "tolerance." They are sure to be disappointed—egalitarians will allow no separate peace. Still, as in the past, Christianity will survive because of its role as a safety valve—and it will continue to modify itself to fit with the *Zeitgeist*.

Of course, most Christians authentically believe in the literal reality of their God—perhaps far more than most "neo-pagans" literally believe in the reality of Wotan or an Earth Goddess. Far from being a strength, this is a weakness. First, the makeup of this "God," far from being unchanging, smoothly modifies itself to fit modern moral standards. Interracial marriage was once condemned as a grave sin against the Creator. Today, the "God" of most Christians is a fuzzy Martin Luther King Jr. in the sky— indeed, King himself is now a "saint" in the Episcopal Church.

Be it the Monarch of the Catholic Magisterium, the personal Jesus of the evangelical, or the divine social worker of the mainline Protestant, God seems to change His nature to fit what the *New York Times* demands— though on some issues he may be a few years late. Does anyone doubt that within a few decades most Christians will be celebrating homosexuality in the same way they celebrate interracial marriage today? The only exceptions will be the literalists such as those at Westboro Baptist Church who themselves serve as proof of Christianity's alienation from reality. Thus the choice for the Christian is either surrender to the culture, or arbitrary allegiance to random Scriptural verses. Yet even the Westboro Baptists hold to a more authentic (and in some ways honorable) form of Christianity by truly believing what their Holy Book tells them, even in defiance of all the world.

Aside from these few marginalized believers and those like them, even the supposedly conservative Christians don't really believe what they say. A true Catholic has to believe that those outside the Church are sentenced to perdition. It was the importance of this belief that allowed Crusaders and conquistadors to slaughter and forcibly convert the heathens and think they were doing good. No one truly believes this today. Even supposedly conservative Christians see no problem with uniting disparate faiths in order to uphold a vague sense of "values," rather than insisting on the correctness of their denomination. Bishop Williamson's denial of the Holocaust was held to be far more sinful by Benedict XVI than the Jews' denial (and arguably, collective murder) of Jesus Christ as Savior.

People were once willing to die—and more importantly, kill—for their faith because believers thought deeply important things were at stake. After all, if Hell is real and one is in possession of the keys to salvation, then tolerating error is the real cruelty. What do the few moments pain suffered by a burning a heretic matter if it gives the unfortunate dissenter eternal bliss? However, in an age of ecumenicism, tolerance, and political correctness, it's hard to imagine that religious leaders believe they have a real claim to Truth. Excommunication, condemnation, and the violent rhetoric of damnation seem reserved only for sins newly discovered after 1945, such as "racism."

Thus, renewing Christian belief is unlikely to "save Western civilization." If anything, it would facilitate the process of conservatives serving as priests of a dead God, guardians of the "West as a tomb" bereft of vitality and spiritual substance.[7] The literate Christian missionaries of yesteryear may well have been a necessary step in advancing the social and technological development of Europe. However, the spiritual unity of what was once called "Christendom" existed even before the coming of Christ, in the dream of Rome and the unity of the Greeks against the barbarians. Europe as a cultural and racial unit existed before Christ, and we do not need Him to maintain it. What the "positive Christianity" of the past contributed to the West was as much a product of European folk tradition and spirituality as the creed of the Nazarene, and if the latter is distilled down to its purest essence, Europe will not survive. If "Christendom" were reborn, the West would simply repeat its past mistake.

The only kind of "Christendom" that could redeem the West is a Germanic Christianity, which is to say, a pagan Christianity drawing upon European folk traditions. Given our history, why must we continue to cling to this unnatural conglomeration? What we need to do is not continue to shock life into a dead God (and a foreign one at that), but establish a link with Primordial Tradition that can speak to worker and philosopher, scientist and mystic. We can tap into those things that made Christianity the faith of the West and discard those things that have led our people to the brink of extinction. The cathedrals, spiritual lessons, and Crusades of our folk will always be a source of inspiration. But they speak to us because they are an expression of *us*—not because of the creed they supposedly championed.

---

[7] http://www.theoccidentalobserver.net/2011/10/the-west-as-a-tomb/

Hilaire Belloc famously wrote, "The Faith is Europe, and Europe is the Faith." He is right, but not in the sense he intended. The Faith *was* Europe, and the folk traditions that built the Germanized Christianity of our forebears. Today, we must renew that faith, a faith of, for, and about the European folk soul. We must discard the distractions and rediscover the living spiritual practices of our folk and their connection to Primordial Tradition. What Christianity supposedly gave us, we already possessed. What Christianity costs us, we can no longer afford.

Counter-Currents/*North American New Right*,
July 31, 2013

No Separate Peace:
Religious Conservatives & the
White Right

It's staggering to realize how universally accepted racial realism once was and how many people are alive who
remember those times. In some ways, it's encouraging.
Walking the earth today are Marines of the segregated
Corps that fought a race war in the Pacific, Southerners
who participated in "massive resistance" to desegregation, and Irish-Americans who fought in the streets of
South Boston to preserve their school system. All of this
is condemned by today's court historians, but only the
most fanatical progressive would unhesitatingly condemn their own grandparents as "Nazis" or soulless racists. For the younger generation, there exists a sense of
amazement that there was once a time when people
could openly discuss racial issues without looking over
their shoulders in fear and trembling.

Of course, today's Americans are living through a similar shift in public opinion regarding the issue of homosexuality. All but universally condemned a generation
ago, today homosexuality is championed as a positive
good by most media outlets and celebrity culture. Even
someone's choice of fast food is now a matter of the ut-
most seriousness, as eating a Chik-fil-A sandwich has
become a political statement. It was only in 2003 when
anti-sodomy laws were ruled unconstitutional by the US
Supreme Court, and it was President Bill Clinton, hardly
a champion of "family values," who signed the Defense of
Marriage Act, which pledged the federal government to
defend matrimony as between one man and one woman.

In cultural terms, the shift is even more dramatic, as
the media increasingly pushes images of same-sex rela-

tionships. Whereas Religious Right candidates of only a few years past would use shock images of two males kissing as an outrageous provocation to rally Christian voters, today the automatons running culture dispensers like *The Huffington Post* or *Gawker* enthusiastically show pictures of men kissing and tell Americans that it is sexy. Whereas a staple of comedy only a few years ago was the disgusted reaction of a male who mistakenly kissed another man (such as Jim Carrey in *Ace Ventura*), we can be sure that future generations will view such scenes with loathing and outrage in the same way that we are all supposed to be deeply upset about Bugs Bunny cartoons mocking the Japanese from World War II.

The specifics are not important. What's important is that we are living through a dramatic shift in public attitudes equivalent to that which took place during the so-called Civil Rights Movement. In real time, we are witnessing how quickly, easily, and automatically media and financial pressure can utterly transform what were once the bedrock values of a society. We are witnessing the destruction of the idea that mass culture has anything to do with choice.

There are obvious potential conflicts between racial realism and social conservatism as regards traditional marriage. While most white advocates tend to be social conservatives who oppose homosexuality, others would consider the issue unimportant. Even conservative White Nationalists would generally consider racial questions more crucial than private sexual behavior. White advocates influenced by the European New Right might even argue for moving beyond the "reactionary" sexual demands of conservative Christianity, including restraints on sexual behavior. While most of this focuses on the controversy over "game" or the imperative of alpha males to regain their masculinity in a feminist culture, others have explicitly argued that intolerance of homosexuality is itself a sign of hostile cultural distortion, and that transcending homophobia would be a victory.

For their part, conservative American Christians may be the only actual racial egalitarians in the entire world. While the fetishization of fashionable minorities is a status symbol for most whites, conservative Christians have legitimately constructed a subculture where religion trumps race and ethnicity.

Hostility towards evolution and sociobiology have given many evangelical Christians a formidable ideological defense against any theory that would distinguish the races of mankind or explain their development.

Furthermore, as salvation is not a question of correct practice or heritage but of correct belief, all men are equal in the sight of God, with differences of birth held to be unimportant.

Going further, non-whites may actually be superior, because their difficult life makes them more receptive to walking through the open door of salvation, while rich whites sinfully ignore their opportunity.

It's therefore not surprising to see the graduates of overwhelmingly white conservative Christian colleges or the pastors of white congregations remain indifferent to their own racial dispossession while enthusiastically proselytizing, contributing to, or even adopting Third World populations.

As regards homosexuality, this kind of Third World fetishism has been made explicit. "Pro-family" organizations and spokespeople in the United States have vocally supported anti-homosexual legislation in nations such as Uganda. Social conservatives have also attempted to use non-whites as a way to build an international coalition against the more permissive Western world. As Christian belief is more important than all other loyalties, it is entirely logical for conservative Episcopalians to rally to the authority of African archbishops rather than that of Canterbury, or for conservative Christians to accuse white liberals of "racism" for not recognizing the right of black Africans to execute homosexuals.

Nonetheless, despite it all, conservative Christians and white advocates (even the most anti-Christian and sexually permissive) share a common fate. In recent years, the Southern Poverty Law Center has taken to labeling formerly "mainstream" political pressure groups such as the Family Research Council as "hate groups." The ever-shifting goalposts of "hate" are not new, as anti-racist and politically well-connected groups such as the Federation for American Immigration Reform (FAIR) or ProEnglish have already been labeled hate groups. What is different is the breakaway from issues that can at least be tangentially connected to race and demographics into sexuality. Undoubtedly for financial reasons, the SPLC and other such groups have decided that even sexual violations of the egalitarian principle are to be punished with social destruction.

The parallel to the struggle against desegregation is obvious. Initially, almost all of the legitimate institutions of the Southern states rose in "massive resistance" to the idea of integration with blacks and public opinion was on the side of "racists." Prince Edward County in Virginia even went so far as to abolish its public school system.

Openly racial groups flourished, as well as more moderate conservatives who created all sorts of silly rationalizations to avoid the real issue. This included the Jew Milton Friedman arguing in *Capitalism and Freedom* that Virginians had suddenly become libertarians when they privatized schools or, slightly more defensibly, William F. Buckley arguing in the pages of *National Review* that white Southerners, as the more "advanced" race, had the right to protect themselves.

However, the usual combination of Left-wing activism and capitalist hostility to white racial (and thus interclass) unity broke the segregationist coalition but left the "Right" dependent on an almost entirely white base.

In the face of cultural disintegration, white conservative Christians transitioned from segregationists into color-blind activists of the Religious Right. In some cases, this was a clumsy and deliberate transition. Jerry Falwell, who once explicitly defended segregation as "God's will," smoothly reinterpreted the eternal teachings of the Almighty when it became untenable and drew new lines in the sand on abortion and homosexuality. Jesse Helms, who built his career as a commentator defending segregation and condemning the "irresponsibility of Negroes," similarly reinvented himself as a conservative Christian. However, despite these and many other examples, the transition for many conservative Christians (especially white Southerners) was unconscious.

As James Kirkpatrick points out, drawing on the work of Sam Francis, conservative white Christians suffered from a "false consciousness," substituting religious militancy to fill the vacuum of cultural breakdown. Sam Francis noted that the real motivation of the Religious Right was:

> [T]he perception . . . that the culture their religion reflects and defends is withering and that that withering portends a disaster for themselves, their class, their country, and their civilization. Religion happens to be a convenient vehicle for their otherwise unarticulated and perfectly well founded fears.[1]

Alas, ideas have consequences, and whatever the root cause of this political movement, the practical conse-

---

[1] http://www.alternativeright.com/main/blogs/untimely-observations/the-great-unawakening/

quences were predictable. The Southern Baptists are now led by a black man and are changing their name to be avoid being called "racists"; Helms ended his career capering around The Dark Continent with Bono talking about the need for more AIDS funding; and religious conservatives can be found shilling for open borders on the grounds that virtuous mestizos will be a useful check on the evil secular whites enjoying craft beer in godless and wealthy cities.

An implicitly white but explicitly anti-white subculture was also a useful ally for conservative movement politicos who needed a way to keep working-class whites voting Republican without having to confront the problems of multiculturalism or (even worse) look after their economic interests by supporting immigration restriction or protectionism. Thus, the Religious Right has deep roots within the official conservative movement, with the Beltway Right formally aligned with multimillion-dollar foundations and donors that cannot be easily dismissed. While conservatives were able to simply wish away their prior opposition to civil rights and even go so far as to claim they came up with the idea, it will be far more difficult to push away the Christians and their unfashionable opinions.

A homosexual activist threw this into stark relief by shooting a security guard at the Family Research Council. The President of the Council, the consummate politico Tony Perkins, explicitly blamed the Southern Poverty Law Center for creating the climate of intimidation that led to the shooting. Many stalwarts of the conservative movement also joined in with forthright criticism of the SPLC, calling it simply a progressive attack dog. This builds on the prior defense of the FRC by Republican politicians (including now Speaker of the House John Boehner) and staffers from conservative groups such as the Media Research Center, which rallied around the cry

"Start Debating, Stop Hating."

However, lest white advocates be encouraged, proponents of traditional values were not outraged at the institution of the SPLC itself. Instead, they were angry that they were lumped in with the icky defenders of their white constituency. The typical spin was that the Southern Poverty Law Center was noble, even heroic when fighting the Ku Klux Klan and the dire threat of American Nazis. Now, however, they had "gone too far."

The most recent highlight is an indignant whine scribbled by perennial pubescent Rich Lowry, whose cherubic and innocent visage matches his political sophistication but conceals the reality that he's a middle-aged man. William F. Buckley appointed Lowry editor of *National Review* in a characteristic fit of absence of mind, after the latter had already dismissed Joseph Sobran and demoted John O'Sullivan and Peter Brimelow.

Lowry has never written anything of lasting importance, and his prose has not graduated from the conservatism-by-the-numbers style taught by Beltway Right institutions to socially maladjusted college students. By aping Republican talking points and taking care never to delve into forbidden territory, they can guarantee at least some form of a living in the American Right's own unique form of affirmative action.

Alas, occasionally an independent thinker sneaks past the defenses and writes something unauthorized. Thus it was that earlier this year that Rich Lowry terminated John Derbyshire for saying sensible things about avoiding black crime, thus returning *National Review* to more serious concerns like posting pictures of his dead cat. He also terminated Jewish writer Robert Weissberg for the dire crime of speaking to an *American Renaissance* convention, and actually took care to *thank* the Left-wing commissars who alerted him. Proudly, avowedly, unabashedly, Lowry knows the role of American conservatives—to be good losers so they can argue with lesbians like Rachel Maddow on *Meet the Press* about things that don't matter. Lowry went on to write masterpieces of conservative prose like "Al Sharpton is Right."

Unfortunately, Lowry has to go through at least the pretense of defending traditional social beliefs once in a while. Therefore, he prissily moaned that the Left was being "intolerant" and "illiberal" to the Family Research Council, and was guilty of a "bullying attempt to short-circuit free debate."[2] This was bad, but not because shutting down free debate is wrong. In fact, Lowry takes care to note that when it comes to racism, "the SPLC brags about shutting down such groups, and rightly so." Hilariously, he then acts the tough guy and notes, "You presumably don't have an argument with the White Patriot Party militia, unless you bring along a lead pipe."

Now, if someone actually attacked one of these groups with a lead pipe, the only real result is you would probably be charged with assaulting a federal employee. Moreover, the idea that Lowry could even lift a lead pipe, never mind wield it, is far-fetched, and the idea that "antifa" would regard him as anything other than an enemy is even more absurd. Of course, an actual fight between Rich Lowry and a typical "antifa" would be a slap fight only mildly less pathetic than a riot at a convention for *My Little Pony*.

That said, let's give Lowry some credit. He proudly and overtly wants to maintain the double standard that opposition to gay marriage is worthy of public debate while opposition to white genocide is not. Lest I be accused of exaggeration, Lowry gives an example of what he regards as hateful extremism by saying, "The home page of the Aryan Nation features an appeal to 'white

---

[2] http://www.nationalreview.com/articles/314531/splc-s-intolerant-campaign-rich-lowry

Americans' to fight anti-white genocide in South Africa, along with a photo of Nelson Mandela standing next to 'the Jew Joe Slovo.'"

Thanks to Lowry, we can all be relieved that apparently "white genocide" in South Africa isn't happening, and observers such as Genocide Watch on the Left and conservative columnist (and Jewess) Ilana Mercer on the Right are just making things up. The scare quotes around "white Americans" is another nice touch by Lowry, who never seems quite as skeptical about terms such as "African Americans." Seeing as how recent polls suggest that Mitt Romney is quite literally receiving zero percent of the, ahem, "African American" vote, the "Party of Civil Rights" has some work to do. It must just be that racist liberal media.

There is something more here though. While perhaps the phrasing the "Jew Joe Slovo" was a trifle indelicate, it is also a fact that Slovo was a leader of the South African Communist Party and a key supporter of Mandela (as well as being, of course, a Jew). It's also worth noting that most conservatives considered Mandela a terrorist, with a youth group of UK Conservative Party members even calling for Mandela's execution. It's also for that reason that American conservatives generally opposed sanctions against South Africa, most notably Ronald Reagan. Finally, the vast majority of American conservatives considered the African National Congress victory a disaster because it handed over strategic territory to the Soviet Union. One almost hesitates to add that it was not just the British who called Nelson Mandela a murderous terrorist who deserved jail time. It was also William F. Buckley—in the pages of *National Review*.[3]

There is no doubt that despite Lowry's stupidity and

---

[3] http://www.vdare.com/articles/mandelas-example-for-obama

cowardice, he will be condemned by his spiritual descendants as the equivalent of a segregationist in whatever form *National Review* limps on in the future. As Lowry's (and more broadly, the conservative movement's) defense of the Family Research Council as "legitimate" is not based in principle but on momentary respectability, it is doomed to be abandoned as the egalitarian revolution rolls on. The only thing that can be said in American conservatism's defense is that it is extremely good at neglecting its own past. We can be sure that whatever nonentity is administering *National Review*'s continuing losses of millions of dollars in 2050 will be claiming that conservatives actually invented the idea of gay marriage.

Where, however, does that leave Christian conservatives? While in the short term, persecution has strengthened their position, the long-term trends are not good. The real balance of power within the conservative movement and the Republican Party lies with those who control the money, and Wall Street financiers and party insiders (some of whom are gay themselves, such as Ken Mehlman) have formed an alliance to push the party away from its socially conservative base. It should also be noted that Jewish money, like that of Republican megadonor Sheldon Adelson, is focused on guaranteeing unconditional American support for Israel, rather than any religious concerns for the *goyim*. It can be expected that the GOP will all but abandon traditional marriage as an issue within the decade, no doubt proclaiming it as a victory.

This essentially leaves the Christian conservative rump within the GOP with two choices. The first is to do what they did with race and simply change the eternal principles of the faith to go with the times. Gay marriage will thus be reinterpreted as a new form of Christian love just as miscegenation went from an abomination to an expression of divine favor. The pro-life cause, especially its fetishization of non-white births, will give whatever rump Religious Right is left enough rationale to keep fundraising, organizing, and employing itself. However, this would require frank surrender on issues of homosexuality and sexual conduct more broadly.

The second choice is that, almost despite themselves, conservative Christians will be forced into the same camp as racial realists and white advocates. Once respectable or even unanimous views will be regarded as simply unfit for consideration by decent society. While many Christian denominations will simply go along with the *Zeitgeist* and so be suffered to exist in the same way as mainline Protestants or Unitarian Universalists, it can be expected that at least some conservative denominations will attempt to survive as something more than inner city charities. Unlike White Nationalists (at least until now), a faith tradition actually has the ability to forge a self-sustaining community, and not all churches will be so quick to abandon the Great Commission to convert the world and live what they see as a Christian life.

When analyzing contemporary faith from an outsider's perspective, it's important to remember that the many millions of evangelical Christians in the United States *really believe* in their faith and that their loyalty to Christ is more important than anything else in their lives. While Christian teachings on sexuality, race, or politics can be warped or subverted, there will always be a substantial population of Christians that at least hold to the tenet that literal belief in the godhood of Christ is necessary for salvation.

In and of itself, this has no temporal importance. It may even encourage passivity, as Christians are tempted to believe that God will somehow save them from the worldly destruction of their faith, literally pulling a *deus ex machina* to prove to everyone else that the Christians had it right all along. For that reason, revolutionaries of both Left and Right have argued that Christianity is an ideal religion for the passive, a "slave morality" that encourages people to lead quiet lives and show compassion rather than righteously overthrow their worldly oppressors. From this perspective, the destruction of the white West is simply Christianity taken to its logical conclusion of self-annihilation. One might even expect our rulers to tolerate or welcome Christianity as a harmless spiritual outlet for a broken people.

Of course, this expected reaction is the precise opposite of what is happening. Even as Christianity becomes ever weaker in public life, the shrieks of hatred and loathing from the secular Left grow in intensity and fervor. Egalitarianism is like the Borg, ruthlessly assimilating all that is in its path and transforming whatever cultural forms it encounters into itself.

It's all very well to write that "Christianity is the grandfather of Marxism" or that egalitarianism derives from Christian morality, Protestant heresies, or the Jewish Culture of Critique. It may even be true. None of this changes the fact that a Christian truly believes that he possesses the path to real salvation, that his God really exists, and that He has certain expectations for moral behavior. This alone is reason enough for real Christianity to be suppressed under the Open Society.

"Democracy" is a regime far more insidious and totalitarian in its way than Stalinism. The worst the KGB could do was kill you, without breaking down what constituted your identity. One could die defiant, as an individual or as a community. Under "freedom," the iron triangle of hostile media, financial power, and the occasional fist of state repression smash apart folk and religious communities into a collection of deracinated individuals.

The man is emptied, and then refilled with the approved opinions of a manufactured culture. Separated, powerless, alone, "free individuals" consume media products, work as tax slaves, engage in pointless sexual debauchery, die, and count themselves lucky for their liberty.

Real religion with actual believers is a dire threat to this system because it demands a higher loyalty and constitutes a greater authority than anything the System can produce. Even for unbelievers or outright anti-Christians of the European New Right, traditional Christianity should be seen as a last bastion of resistance and the last subculture not fully under System control.

Certainly, the System views Christians in this way, especially in regards to racial matters. Whatever its tenets, the existence of a subculture based on faith and tradition necessarily falls into certain patterns that violate the egalitarian impulse. In American Christian communities white women are encouraged to stay home and have large families at an early age, and men are told to own their role as masculine protectors. Divorce is discouraged, and while there is plenty of hypocrisy, this is far preferable to the outright celebration of familial annihilation prized by feminists and many secularists. While White Nationalists are debating "game" and battles between the sexes, white Christians have already received answers to these questions and have moved on to having children. Significantly, Left-wing critiques of Christianity (which mostly consist of obscenities or sneering curses) quickly veer into condemnations of white racism. This is, of course, partially true, as at least in a demographic sense, white Christians are doing the most to ensure the physical survival of the Aryan race.

More importantly, Christians possess the only existing counterculture. Churches are a framework for social life that is outside media and government control. Concerts and films of increasing quality allow Christians to get around the messages promoted by Hollywood. A rapidly expanding homeschooling network allows Christian parents to resist indoctrination. It's not that conservative Christians are necessarily promoting positive values. It's that conservative Christians are the one large group that even have the potential to promote these values.

Ideally, loyalty to God, family, folk, and nation should all be one and the same, and the thrilling victories of authentically Christian peoples such as the Afrikaners of the Day of the Vow or the Christian South of Jackson and Lee suggest that whatever the ideological tensions between the Christian faith and the racial folk, they have coexisted successfully in the past. Only with the merger of the divine, familial, ethnic, and political can a people survive in a hostile world.

It's not surprising that in the past, groups like the Family Research Council aligned with groups like the Council of Conservative Citizens in the same way that David Duke linked his political ambitions to Christianity. In less degenerate times, such an alliance seemed natural. Of course, today, this is held as further proof of evil. Rebecca Schoenkopf of *Wonkette* (and yes, I hate to offend Rich Lowry, but she too is some Communist Jew still bitter that her ancestors were chased out of the *shtetls* of Poland) sneered that such alliances make the FRC the same as the Klan. She's right, though not in the way she meant.[4]

Ultimately, if conservative Christians are to survive as a community, they will need to defend themselves as a conscious tribal grouping rather than as a collection of atomized individuals. The power of faith or an appeal to reason won't do them any good, any more than it saved the far more pious Orthodox who prayed fervently before

---

[4] http://wonkette.com/481580/anti-gay-group-leader-frothing-over-hate-group-label-was-totally-gay-married-to-david-duke

the terrible conquest of Byzantium. American conservatism will eventually turn on believing Christians for the same reason it has turned on "racism." The American Right and Left both share the quintessential American impulse towards equality and the furious hostility towards anything that gets in the way of an Open Society of profit-seeking individuals. As the Leftist Noam Chomsky wrote:

> Capitalism basically wants people to be interchangeable cogs, and differences among them, such as on the basis of race, usually are not functional. I mean, they may be functional for a period, like if you want a super-exploited workforce or something, but those situations are kind of anomalous. Over the long term, you can expect capitalism to be anti-racist—just because it's anti-human. And race is in fact a human characteristic—there's no reason why it should be a *negative* characteristic, but it is a human characteristic. So therefore identifications based on race interfere with the basic ideal that people should be available just as consumers and producers, interchangeable cogs who will purchase all the junk that's produced— that's their ultimate function, and any other properties they might have are kind of irrelevant, and usually a nuisance.[5]

Religion, race, and culture are the things that make human beings truly human and that can forge deracinated people into *a* people. If Christianity is going to survive as a community, as opposed to a lifestyle choice akin to veganism or being a "Juggalo," its survival is linked to the

---

[5] http://www.newrightausnz.com/2005/11/28/big-business-as-a-supporter-of-anti-racism-noam-chomsky/

survival of other traditional loyalties. Tradition has to stand against money, blood against gold. No matter what its premises or where its internal logic leads, the survival of any kind of a traditional community, even the most barebones version of low church Protestant Christianity, is impossible in a soulless McWorld run on the principles of 365 Black.

It doesn't matter that the first principles of White Nationalists and committed Christians have nothing in common. It doesn't matter that most conservative Christians are anti-white or at best indifferent to ethnicity, except for worshipping Jews. It doesn't matter that White Nationalists are opposed to almost everything most evangelical Christians stand for. It doesn't even matter that it is the mission of the European (and North American) New Right to tear out egalitarianism by the roots, even if that eventually means Christianity itself. The survival of the white race and the survival of the church on earth require the same kind of cultural and (eventually) political rebellion against the current System. Both of these forces have no choice but to unite for its overthrow. The survival of any kind of authentic belief, tradition, or humanity requires Revolution. The other debates can come later.

Counter-Currents/*North American New Right*,
August 23, 2012

WHY LIBERALS HATE GUNS

THE DEMONIZATION OF GUN OWNERS

"In light of recent events, I'm really concerned about your safety. So for your birthday, I bought you a pistol. It's relatively small caliber, features a safety, great for a beginner. I also bought you some lessons from a qualified instructor so you can get your concealed carry permit. Happy birthday!"

Consider the above. Many of us can think of friends, spouses, or significant others who would be delighted—indeed staggered—by such a generous gift. However, it's not difficult to think of others who would be offended, outraged, or even sickened by it. With the effortless uniformity of thought and action characteristic of North Korean mass games or a typical sociology class, progressives are rejoicing that they have found a white shooter in Newton, Connecticut, so they can try to disarm the American people. Accompanying the political posturing and concern trolling by the likes of sinister clown Joe Biden is a hate campaign against gun owners as inherently dangerous, unstable, and even unpatriotic.

Whites who don't favor the active genocide of their own race are used to being demonized as "racists." Progressives exposed to something as uncontroversial as racial differences in intelligence simply reply with moral outrage and priggish posturing ("I have to take a shower," and so forth). Inanimate objects are now creating the same kind of reaction. Like Victorian hysterics, progressives now blanche, swoon, and vapor at the very thought of people owning guns they don't "need."

A relative at Christmas, unaware that I own several firearms, blithely commented that "Only the police should have guns. Gun owners are crazy and dangerous and should be in jail, to protect the rest of us." Concealed carry permit holders, who are far less likely to commit crimes than the general population, are charged with secretly lusting to murder children. Meanwhile, the Left, operating, as always, without irony, is merrily tweeting away death threats to their political opponents.

I've written elsewhere that the Left's current campaign against guns is closely linked to its overall anti-white agenda.[1] The current debate has been refreshingly frank about the use of firearms by whites to defend against non-white crime. The Left simply charges that whites have a duty to die as a form of penance for past sins against egalitarianism. However, what is occurring is something broader than the usual genocidal impulse against the hated white male. The progressive reaction to Newtown reveals that the utopian impulse at the heart of the modern Left is the desire to escape responsibility itself.

RIGHTS, NOT DUTIES

The end of responsibility is really the end of citizenship. Back when America was a real country, citizenship was a duty owed to the larger society. A citizen is a member of the political community who enjoys certain guarantees in exchange for fulfilling various responsibilities. In a republic, each full citizen has a public role. At the time the Second Amendment was written, the armed defense of the country was held to be a responsibility of the citizen, harkening back to the Germanic conception of the right to bear arms as the key indicator of both freedom and at least some political authority.

Today, citizenship is a burden, offering punishment and censure rather than full participation in political life. The founding stock of the country is actively discrimi-

---

[1] http://www.amren.com/news/2012/12/whites-and-guns/

nated against in jobs, education, and financial aid, and is utterly cut off from meaningful political participation in many of the nation's largest cities on account of our race. Meanwhile, immigrants and their advocates protest that they are "second-class citizens" when in actuality they are not citizens at all. As recipients of free medical care, tax exemptions, state-sponsored ethnic solidarity, and a vast system of patronage and welfare set up for their benefit, those who are not part of the political community are more assiduously courted than actual Americans. The vote is an all but meaningless privilege, for, even if votes are counted, elections lead to results exactly opposed to what voters say they supported.

The reason this is tolerated is because being part of a people is a duty that white progressives do not want. The mark of adulthood is taking responsibility for both one's own support and the continuation of one's line and (it follows) the larger folk of which one is a part. This is no longer a societal expectation. Indeed, it's practically immoral. Diana West notes in *The Death of the Grown-Up* that the very concept of the "teenager" free from adult responsibility is a modern invention, and the definition of teenager now seems to be extending into the twenties and thirties. It is no accident that this coincides with the rise of racial egalitarianism in the West.

Whatever the intents of the Founding Fathers, the mistake of ascribing "self-evident" and "inalienable" rights to individuals *qua* individuals undermined the very republican virtues needed to sustain the experiment. The premise of classical liberalism is that each person is autonomous, equal in some cosmic sense, and ideally unburdened by any tradition or restriction upon his or her sacred "choice." The problem is that Man in the abstract, as Joseph de Maistre observed, is a creature that does not exist. After the promises of the Declaration of Independence, which even the slave-owning, white supremacist founders did not really believe, any limitations imposed by culture, history, location, family, and nature itself became tyrannical.

Of course, once you've liberated yourself from an organic society, you've also liberated yourself from any concrete loyalties or responsibilities. If the purpose of life is the pursuit of "happiness" through freely chosen obligations, any kind of "duty" rankles. Why should a deracinated individual care whether his line continues? Why should it be his job to bear arms for the state (or against the state, as the case may be) when he could be making money? Indeed, as long as technology and economic circumstances permit, why shouldn't the accumulation of belongings and pleasurable sensations proceed for the entirety of one's life, unencumbered by any restrictions?

Unfortunately, limitations do exist. The story of modern liberalism is the rebellion against these limitations, with the glorious victories against discrimination by race, sex, age, national origin, sexual preference, physical status, appearance, and other facts of life serving as the Stations of the Cross for the new progressive litany. The latest frontier is the rebellion against gender identification, as progressives who refuse to say they are men or women seek to trump Nature, the ultimate Fascist. This is not some crazy liberal scheme, but the logical conclusion of the very founding principles that Glenn Beck blubbers about on his internet channel each night.

Of course, as equality and the demands for unencumbered choice are defined more broadly, state power is required to enforce the ever-expanding mandates. An army of academics, lawyers, and subsidized "activists" are also on hand to document prior incidents of "privilege" that the government must ameliorate in order to ensure equality of opportunity. Thus, a business owner's decision about whom to hire, a joke told at lunch, or the establishment of gender-segregated toilets suddenly become matters of urgent public concern, with legislation, lawsuits, and punitive action following in the wake of each new step towards equality. The quest for individual liberation culminates in an almost unlimited expansion of government, as every business, personal, sexual, or even romantic interaction must be carefully regulated by all the powers of the state.

GUNS, "FREEDOM," THE NEW CLASS, & SOCIAL CONTROL

On the surface, guns are actually a step towards equality. Guns give the physically weak a way to defend against the strong, as neuroscientist and pop intellectual Sam Harris has described. A world without guns is not a more peaceful world, but a more savage one, where brute strength allows bullies to exploit people incapable of fighting back.

Nonetheless, Leftists oppose guns at a primal level because they provide a way for citizens to exercise power without going through their managerial state. Since the rise of the New Class described by James Burnham, political power in the West has not rested so much on religion or even money but on the ability to regulate behavior. Americans are ruled by a whole system of administrators based in courts and bureaucracies that mandate and enforce through state power what forms social interactions may take. With their apologists in the media and academia and control of credentials and licensing, the "managerial class" can regulate everyday behavior more totally than any king. Minorities and the various victim classes are invaluable because they provide both the justification and ideological support to maintain the political class.

What does this mean in everyday life? It means that you know, instinctively, that if the wrong person sees something you wrote, overhears a joke, misinterprets a comment, or just feels like destroying you, there's nothing you can do about it. The tyranny of the New Class is why there are certain situations that you instinctively steer clear of, because there is no way you can win. You know the System is against you.

More importantly, in a life or death situation, the System is far more concerned with protecting itself than protecting you. It's not just that "When seconds count, the police are minutes away." It's that it's better to commit a crime than actually punish the criminal yourself. The entire network of human rights, constitutional guarantees, and all the rest are a way for the state to criminalize attempts at self-protection. Make no mistake—the horror stories from Britain of robbers suing homeowners for attacking them is not a system out of control. It's a system operating precisely as it was designed to.

The case of George Zimmerman and Trayvon Martin is instructive. At this point, it is beyond dispute that Zimmerman was actually attacked. However, Leftists argue that he never should have approached Martin to begin with. The fact that he was a "neighborhood watchmen" only makes it worse; Zimmerman was "untrained" and committed a dire offense by trying to enforce social order himself rather than relying on the police. The failure of the police to stop repeated (and reported) criminal activity over a period of months is irrelevant. It's precisely because Zimmerman did his job effectively that he should be punished.

A gun allows a citizen to take responsibility for his own security and the security of his family. To a Leftist, this is frightening because it means that a person is acting without ideological supervision. Leftist demands for "training," "education," and "licensing," in guns and most everything else is simply a way of asserting dominance over uncontrolled social interactions. In the modern context, "freedom" does not mean freedom to act without restriction on your own property or to interact with others provided you don't violate their basic rights. Instead, "freedom" means the right to act only in accordance with government-determined social norms.

PERMANENT CHILDHOOD

What's this all leading to? A kind of permanent childhood. The citizen is relieved of his duty to protect the political community, protect his family, and protect himself. If anything, he's actually discouraged from having a family or any kind of loyalty beyond himself, as even institutions like churches or civic organizations like the Boy Scouts are viewed with suspicion. All mediating forces between the now powerless individual and the managerial Leviathan are to be stripped away.

The reward is a life free of responsibility. Paradoxically, as the state grows in power, its expectations of the individual decrease. It's absurd to imagine the government today rallying the "militia," because the average American would be incapable or unwilling to respond. Instead, citizens of a modern democracy can live their lives knowing that every product they buy, service they use, or group they participate in has been carefully registered and licensed by state authorities. Eventually, as in Europe, this will extend even to ideas they may hear, or, as in the workplace already, conversations they may have. This is an attractive vision for Last Men. It removes the obligation to have to think about politics, about the future of the community, or about anything other than consumption. As Alexis de Tocqueville predicted in *Democracy in America* in 1831:

> I wish to imagine under what new features despotism might appear in the world: I see an innumerable crowd of men, all alike and equal, turned in upon themselves in a restless search for those petty, vulgar pleasures with which they fill their souls.

Each of them, living apart, is almost unaware of the destiny of all the rest. His children and personal friends are for him the whole of the human race; as for the remainder of his fellow citizens, he stands alongside them but does not see them; he touches them without feeling them; he exists only in himself and for himself; if he still retains his family circle, at any rate he may be said to have lost his country. . . . Above these men stands an immense and protective power which alone is responsible for looking after their enjoyments and watching over their destiny. It is absolute, meticulous, ordered, provident, and kindly disposed. It would be like a fatherly authority, if, fatherlike, its aims were to prepare men for manhood, but it seeks only to keep them in perpetual childhood; it prefers its citizens to enjoy themselves provided they have only enjoyment in mind. It works readily for their happiness but it wishes to be the only provider and judge of it. It provides their security, anticipates and guarantees their needs, supplies their pleasures, directs their principal concerns, manages their industry, regulates their estates, divides their inheritances. Why can it not remove them entirely from the bother of thinking and the troubles of life?[2]

Therefore, the only freedoms that are allowed are ones that further "enjoyment." There's a reason why Prohibition of alcohol has become unthinkable even as prohibition of guns is now debated. Certainly, alcohol kills more people than guns. Alcohol also provides no con-

---

[2] Alexis de Tocqueville, *Democracy in America and Two Essays on America*, trans. Gerald E. Bevan, ed. Isaac Kramnick (New York: Penguin, 2003), p. 805.

crete benefits beyond pleasure, whereas a gun can save someone's life. Alcohol, like guns, can be dangerous in the wrong hands. Nonetheless, Americans accept beer commercials on TV in a way they would never accept rifle commercials precisely because the product is an amusement, an anesthetization against adult action. It doesn't remove power from the managerial state or question the moral basis of the System in the same way as gun ownership. An addict is tolerated, even coddled by our society. A responsible gun owner is feared.

Our system relieves a person of having to suffer moral responsibility for anything. The decisions have already been made. Thus we have black progressive Ta-Nehisi Coates admitting that since he knows he will die someday, he would rather be shot than own a firearm and take the power of life and death upon himself.[3] It is literally better to die—better even to let one's children die—than be armed.

As Lawrence Auster points out, to kill is the ultimate act of discrimination, because it involves the value judgment that *my* life and the lives of those I love are more important than the life of another. While gun owners are stigmatized as "fearful," it's actually progressives who seem to be trembling at the thought of white people who don't go along with the program. As Nietzsche said, "No shepherd and one herd! Everybody wants the same, everybody is the same: whoever feels different goes voluntarily into a madhouse."[4]

Or in our version, you get forced into the playhouse. Alcohol, perverted sexuality, video games, and all the

---

[3] http://www.theatlantic.com/national/archive/2012/12/more-guns-less-crime-a-dialogue/266576/

[4] Friedrich Nietzsche, *Thus Spoke Zarathustra*, in *The Portable Nietzsche*, ed. and trans. Walter Kaufmann (New York: Penguin, 1954), p. 130.

rest are simply blocks for big kids. The adults of the economic and financial elite make the big decisions, but you get to run around with toys and not have to worry about anything. "Freedom" in this sense is the freedom to play.

Gun owners are proof that people can exist and survive outside the managerial state's system of control. As with homeschoolers, traditional religious communities, and, well, "racists," guns present a greater moral danger to the Left than a physical danger. When the people are disarmed, it does not mean that insurrection suddenly becomes impossible because the military equation has changed. It means that insurrection is impossible because psychologically Americans will have admitted they cannot live without an egalitarian bureaucracy informing them how to behave and what to think, and they will not allow others to do so. Gun owners are hated because they say that playtime is over. We're hated because we say it is time to grow up.

Counter-Currents/*North American New Right*,
January 18, 2013

BELTWAY RAMBOS

Are conservatives going to start shooting people?

The Beltway Right is defending so-called "assault weapons" because they are the final check on government repression. After Alex Jones's typically bombastic performance on Piers Morgan, Breitbart.com contributor and controlled opposition Ben Shapiro appeared to play the "reasonable conservative" across from the C-list celebrity hacker.[1] He argued that the American people need AR-15s because they provide a concrete way to resist the state. Piers Morgan was of course indignant, arguing that the military could easily kill any Americans that dared oppose them.

Let's leave aside the obvious conclusion that the likes of Piers Morgan are fantasizing about the military mowing down conservatives. We already know that progressivism has grown to love the police state. What is more interesting is even the simpering castrati of the Beltway have taken a break from denouncing the "black genocide" of abortion, condemning Nazis like Chuck Hagel, and urging more immigration to indulge in their own dreams of righteous violence.

They are, after all, correct—the Second Amendment, is, as they say, not about deer hunting. As America's military is well into year 11 of the War in Afghanistan against illiterate tribesman armed with antiquated weapons, the likes of Shapiro seem to have a better grasp on the potential of insurgency and guerrilla warfare than Field Marshal Morgan.

That said, even though they're right, what are con-

---

[1] http://www.glennbeck.com/content/blog/show/piers-morgan-gets-owned-by-ben-shapiro-refers-to-constitution-as-your-little-book/

servatives really saying here? Let's spell it out. Resisting government tyranny with rifles means that Americans will someday shoot the servants of the state when some line is crossed. This means killing police officers, soldiers, security personnel, and, presumably, politicians. Forget euphemism: are conservatives willing to say what they are actually proposing?

Of course, a typical American conservative would protest that he's not saying we should shoot people *now*, but at some future point when a line is crossed. Some of my more dedicated libertarian colleagues are fond of saying that "we are at that awkward point where it is too late to work within the system but too early to start shooting the bastards." Fair enough. Who do we shoot and when? Where is the line?

Is it when the government starts telling you what you can do with your property? Well, we haven't had that right since the Civil Rights Act of 1964, and various additions, court rulings, and regulatory expansions have restricted it further. While the abuse of eminent domain hasn't quite reached Chinese levels, the Kelo ruling from the Supreme Court gives government the right to confiscate your property for minimal recompense, in order to help the investments of the rich.

How about government taking your children from you? Well, they can do that. It can be because you lost a divorce case. It can be because the government doesn't like the names you gave them.[2] It can be over your political beliefs.[3] It can be over your religion—assuming they don't just kill your family in order to "protect" them, like they did at Waco and Ruby Ridge. It can even be just for

---

[2] http://hotair.com/archives/2009/01/14/new-jersey-child-services-seizes-boy-named-after-hitler-from-parents/

[3] http://www.prisonplanet.com/government-seizes-newborn-baby-over-political-beliefs-of-parents.html

the hell of it.[4]

How about telling you what you can eat or drink? Well, the government sends armed men to arrest people for drinking raw milk in the land of the free.[5] And don't you dare try to open a lemonade stand.[6]

Shutting down your business and destroying your livelihood? Well, that happens all the time. It can be because of the "environment."[7] It can be because of "racism."[8] It can be because of regulation.[9] It can be because they just don't like you.

Waging wars of aggression based on faulty information? Well . . . conservatives, at least some of them, tend to like that. But yeah, we do that too.

That's it! God! People fight in the name of God. Will the dreaded American Religious Right rise in righteous fury against the Babylon on the Potomac that sanctions infanticide, celebrates gay marriage, and wages unrelenting war against Christianity in the public square? Actually, evangelicals are more likely to die for the Beast, though they are despised by their masters. And the main concern of evangelical leaders right now is that America doesn't have enough Mexicans.

---

[4] http://www.willamettelive.com/2010/news/two-young-parents-face-off-against-dhs-to-regain-custody-of-their-twin-boys/

[5] http://www.theatlantic.com/health/archive/2011/08/the-latest-raw-milk-raid-an-attack-on-food-freedom/243635/

[6] http://www.nationalreview.com/corner/273642/when-obama-hands-you-lemons-mark-steyn

[7] http://www.nationalreview.com/articles/335174/raw-deal-jillian-kay-melchior

[8] http://usnews.nbcnews.com/_news/2012/08/16/13321106-philadelphia-swim-club-discrimination-case-settled?lite

[9] http://theeconomiccollapseblog.com/archives/suffocated-by-red-tape-12-ridiculous-regulations-that-are-almost-too-bizarre-to-believe

What about freedom of speech? It's true that the United States still has the First Amendment. While it is used to defend pornography, obscenity, and various other filth, in theory it should actually protect political speech. In this country, it does. You won't be arrested for saying something politically incorrect. The state will just help your enemies have you fired, threatened, stripped of property, defamed, and physically attacked.

But you won't be arrested. Definitely not. That only happens in dictatorships like Great Britain, France, or Germany, which presumably American conservatives are willing to overthrow.

Arbitrary taxation?[10] Sending "swarms of Officers to harass our people, and eat out their substance"? Hounding people to the grave so the government has more money to give to powerful bankers?[11] Yup, yup, yup.

Ah! Discrimination. We can all agree the oppressed should rise up against that. Well, whites are discriminated against in jobs and education. Schools defame them as a group. Minorities and immigrants receive preferential treatment when starting a business, making it difficult to compete. And the real problem the country faces is . . . white privilege.

Well, at least you can vote your way out. Like when Michigan outlawed affirmative action. Oh wait . . . actually the courts threw that out because they said it would hurt minorities.[12] The law is the law, unless a Leftist says it will make blacks feel sad. Then it doesn't count. So that doesn't work either. Same with Proposition 187 in

---

[10] http://www.theblaze.com/stories/2012/09/28/these-are-the-top-5-worst-taxes-obamacare-will-impose-in-2013/

[11] http://reason.com/archives/1991/03/01/taxes-and-death; http://www.vdare.com/articles/was-the-bailout-itself-a-scam

[12] http://www.vdare.com/posts/by-any-means-necessary-the-obama-victory-and-affirmative-action

California a decade ago.[13] Good thing that immigration never had any bad impacts on California.

Well, there is one thing which definitely serves as the definition of tyranny. If government can seize you, without trial, without charges, without counsel, and then have you killed, that is tyranny.

Oh . . . actually they do that too.[14]

Here's the problem. You have a country where whites are officially discriminated against by the government and have their earnings savaged by taxes and inflation. They work long hours if they are lucky enough to find a job so they can subsidize people who hate them. They send their kids to schools that teach them they are evil. Meanwhile, other laws are openly ignored so non-white immigrants can displace them from jobs, resources, and political power. If, out of desperation, they join the armed services, they will be sent to die in wars fought for the benefit of someone else. In fact, one of the people they are supposed to be fighting "for" will probably be the one who shoots them. And there's no way out.

All of this exists today in what used to be our country. Elsewhere in the Western world, it is actually worse. What is more likely—that *National Review* publishes a call to take up arms or that it pushes a new editorial about how conservatives can win minority voters with talk about the economy?[15]

That said, there is an answer as to when people will finally be ready to start shooting back. People will use their guns against the government . . . when the govern-

---

[13] http://www.vdare.com/articles/proposition-187-victory-in-defeat

[14] http://www.huffingtonpost.com/2012/03/05/us-targeted-killings-eric-holder_n_1320515.html

[15] http://www.nationalreview.com/articles/333327/demography-destiny-thomas-sowell

ment comes to take their guns.

Of course, this has it all backwards. The guns are supposed to protect something other than themselves—property, family, liberty, anything. Instead, Americans are only willing to use their guns in order to defend their guns.

The fact is this country is far more repressive, tyrannical, and totalitarian than anything we revolted against the British for. As James Mason points out about His Majesty George III, "This man could have been called a lot of things, but he couldn't be called evil." The American government, as a collective entity, is evil. Yet here we are, pretending we are free, defending our revolutionary heritage when all of the critical battles have already been fought and lost. If self-government means anything, we've already lost it. If tyranny means anything other than "scary uniforms," it's already here.

Conservatives aren't going to shoot anybody. They soil themselves when someone calls them racist, and we are supposed to believe that they are going to take the "God bless our troops" stickers off their SUVs and start mowing down Marines?

Even though I despise gun-grabbing liberals, let me give them some unsolicited advice. Call conservatives' bluff. Let's have progressives ask conservatives when they think it is right to start killing people. Let's cut the nonsense. Let's see what conservatives actually think they are fighting for and what they think is important. My guess is they don't even know.

Perhaps it is better if they take our guns. At least then the Beltway Right won't have any more excuses. We'll be serfs, but at least we'll be serfs without illusions. Then, maybe, we can do something about it besides bluster.

Counter-Currents/*North American New Right*,
January 15, 2013

TRUMP:
THE LAST AMERICAN

According to its leaders, the American people doesn't really exist. There's something called the United States, a landmass filled with citizens (and uniformly virtuous immigrants) who are hard-working and industrious. This geographic entity is "exceptional" and uniquely blessed by God, as are its swelling numbers of random inhabitants. But there's no nation. Instead, there's a collection of individuals, all "free," united only by certain "principles" and "ideals." And our leaders always say our best days are still before us.

Thus, American politics isn't about securing our interests as a people or a nation. Instead, it is an endless argument about the American Creed, the slogans handed down to us from our founding about freedom and liberty and all men being equal. The Right and Left will emphasize one slogan or the other, but the vocabulary is always the same. And somehow, the more high-minded and abstract the rhetoric, the more comfortably it serves the interests of those who already hold power.

Of course, the historic American nation, the white American core of the polity, keeps the System creaking along, even as this indispensable ethnic group is dispossessed and deconstructed by its own government.

But now, there's a palpable sense the whole thing is breaking down. Income inequality has all but destroyed social mobility, and the middle class is collapsing. Radical social movements undermined traditional values. Ethnic tensions destroyed social trust as the founding population has been gradually pushed aside in the country it created. And basic responsibilities of the state such as the maintenance of infrastructure, border security, and even the administration of justice, are starting to collapse even as the government struggles to hold together a far-flung military empire.

In short, in terms of where we are in the historical development cycle, America is about due for a Caesar. But because this is America, Caesar may arrive in the form of a reality TV star.

Donald Trump promises to Make America Great Again. His appeal, which Peter Brimelow described as "kingly," is revolutionary. It is revolutionary precisely because it dispenses with the usual American Revolutionary rhetoric.

What Donald Trump says could apply to any country. Behind the rhetoric and bravura, the heart of Trump's case is that the United States is being exploited by crafty foreigners and let down by stupid leaders. Our soldiers are used as pawns in overseas military adventures that don't serve our interests. Our workers are being crushed by catastrophic trade agreements. Our future is being given away to immigrants who are taking our country right out from under us. "We have to stop being the stupid country," Trump always says.

This appeal could be made by any other charismatic leader of any other country. Rather than saying America is "exceptional," Trump is saying we are a country like any other, one losing the global competition for power and wealth. There's nothing inherent about America that makes it "great"—it takes decisive action and bold leadership to defeat our enemies and restore our power. Trump makes many conservatives uncomfortable because implicit in his approach is the idea that it's possible for America to lose.

It's possible if he's not the leader anyway. Trump promises a strong and great country we will all be "so proud" to be a part of. "I want to do something very special," he says, as if being the most powerful man in the world will be a sacrifice for him. This will include bringing back the "dignity" of the Office itself. He writes in *Crippled America*: "The president is the spokesperson for democracy and liberty. Isn't it time we brought back the pomp and circumstance, and the sense of awe for that office that we all once held?" Trump is offering himself not just as a problem solver, but as a kind of constitutional monarch and a unifying figure.

But, contra the claims of some of the more excitable elements of Conservatism Inc., Trump's imperial style doesn't make him a dictator. He's promised to work with Democratic leaders and cut deals. For this, he's been attacked by the same conservatives who call him a tyrant in waiting in the next breath.

In his own way, Trump is trying to build a national policy consensus. He says he will provide health care to the poorest among us, which conservatives turned into an accusation of supporting "Obamacare." Unlike many conservatives, Trump has argued against raising the retirement age on Social Security and has no patience for slashing those programs which actually benefit his own supporters. Trump's foreign policy promises an unsentimental defense of our own national interest, rather than the crusading idealism of George W. Bush. When it comes to political correctness, immigration, guns, and taxes, Trump outdoes just about any "movement conservative," but when it comes to spending, he's a moderate who believes in some form of a common good, rather than Margaret Thatcher's sneer that "there is no such thing as society." Rather than that of Ronald Reagan, Trump's conservatism is that of Bismarck.

Interestingly, Trump is appealing to people as Americans—black, white, Hispanic, men, and women. He's using identity politics, but pro-American identity politics, something almost unheard of. He speaks in terms of our collective interest and distinguishes it from the interests of foreigners, whose interests he regards as irrelevant.

When confronted by Left-wing protesters, Trump shakes his head sadly, wondering aloud about those misguided souls who don't want America to be strong and great. Trump is a "citizenist" who views Americans as an organic community to be privileged and protected by "their" government against the *Ausländer* to whom we owe nothing. And we can trust Trump, it's implied, because his massive ego is now identified with that of the nation itself. "My whole life is about winning, and now I want to do that for America," he says.

What's amazing is not how well this is working, but how much trouble he's having. American conservatives have turned on him with savage fury. Their incoherent critique against him largely hinges on Trump's supposed refusal to mouth the usual pieties about "the Constitution" and "freedom" which the Beltway Right doesn't even believe. Trump's tax plan alone shows he is hardly some populist demagogue. While conservatives downplay existential issues like immigration, we are told Trump must be rejected because of his support for ethanol subsidies and eminent domain, both of which will remain in place regardless of who is elected to the Oval Office.

It's also striking how many conservatives have openly said they would rather lose than have him be the nominee. A key talking point of the emerging Alt Right is that the American conservative movement has failed to "conserve" anything important throughout its history, including traditional values, limited government, and the country itself.

Conservatism Inc. has confirmed it is designed to lose. Or more accurately, the Beltway Right believes it is impossible for conservatives to lose. Even if there was a President Bernie Sanders holding court over a 100 percent Socialist Congress, we'd be reading in *National Review* how America is still a "Center-Right nation."

Not only is America not a "Center-Right nation," its

"Right-wing" political tradition seems indifferent to the nation itself. Trump's leading primary challengers, Marco Rubio and Ted Cruz, are not even American in terms of heritage or mindset. Cruz was not born in the country, and for all his recitations of the Constitution, may not even be eligible to be President. To Cruz, the country is simply the subject of a laboratory experiment for his abstract creed of "limited government." Cruz's strange combination of Third World Catholicism and degenerate American evangelism means this Princeton-Harvard lawyer backed by Wall Street money LARPs as a kind of 21st-century Billy Sunday. His crazed father tells the rubes his son is an "anointed king" who will return the nation to God. But Ted seems to have no particular interest in the country he's adopted, viewing it merely as a vehicle for his own ambitions. And his own wife is part of a movement to abolish the country altogether.

While Cruz is indifferent, Rubio is actively hostile to the country's core population. He's assisted major corporations, especially Disney, in replacing his own constituents. He betrayed the conservatives who put him into the office almost moments after winning his election. He's gleeful about plunging the country into another disastrous war in the Middle East, this time against Russia. Rubio represents the return of George W. Bush-style neoconservatism, now with a white Cuban *faux* "Latino" as the *Shabbos goy* instead of a *faux* evangelical cowboy. As with Lindsey Graham, one can't help but suspect "they" have something on him.

Jeb Bush is still in contention, but even a picture of him is self-discrediting. He's simply a caricature of WASP decadence given life.

Conservatives know that neither Cruz nor Rubio would actually do much in office. As Cruz's supporters in Iowa said, they wanted someone who "shares their values." They take the hostility of every person he's ever worked with as proof that he's "principled." Rubio's supporters, especially the consultants, seem to believe he can "win," and what he does after that is essentially irrelevant.

Yet what could a President Trump really do? In the unlikely scenario Trump wins, we'll paper over the hole where our national soul should be with big projects designed to conceal the decline. True, the Great Wall of Trump would be a glorious symbol of our national will to survive. Unfortunately, unless we repatriate post-1965 non-white immigrants, legal and illegal, the demographic damage is already done.

One positive effect is the conservative movement would be reconstituted along nationalist lines. But, without confronting demographic issues directly, there would be almost no way to reverse the underlying causes of American decline. Trump himself has said he would not challenge anti-white racial preferences and, aside from immigration, would leave the multicultural spoils system essentially untouched.

While Trump has undoubtedly fueled the rise of the Alt Right, in office, he might function as a safety valve rather than an accelerant. Like Putin, Trump would impose a vaguely conservative, patriotic veneer on a state with crumbling ethnic foundations. It's not that Trump is "pro-white"; it's that he's not *anti-white*, which makes him far Right in the current political context.

The best that can be said about him is that we don't fully *know* what he'd do, meaning that unlike literally every other candidate, there's at least a chance he won't try make our lives worse. Besides, as every Alt Right supporter of Trump knows, it's not necessarily what the would-be Emperor himself would do, it's what he would lead to—a legitimate, nationalist American Right.

Naturally, American nationalism is far more appealing to European-Americans than White Nationalism. "Whiteness" is a foreign idea to many whites. But we are now in a position where whites are being forcibly enrolled in what is a state church with no salvation. To be white is to be racist, full stop. Granted, many whites (like Elizabeth Warren, for example) will simply stop calling themselves white and suddenly rediscover whatever miniscule non-white heritage they have. Many Hispanics who would have been considered "white" in years past now aggressively demand their membership as part of an "oppressed" group, and other "minorities" are eager to follow suit. Even Asians say they're oppressed now.

But there still need to be some white men left to pay the bills. And as we see with the attempted cleansing of Haitians from the Dominican Republic recently, even when there are no "whites" left, racial tensions don't go away.

The good news is that the System has to force white identity on white Americans, even if they resist it. Concepts like "white privilege" don't work otherwise. The bad news is that the increasingly overt anti-white hysteria is likely to dramatically increase in the years ahead.

Trump reveals, as a Maoist would say, the contradictions within the System. Trump dismisses the propaganda that America is somehow an exception to the laws of history. For America to "win and win and win" as he promises, it requires a nationalist approach in which our government aggressively privileges our own citizens over foreigners.

But that mostly means white people. The dominant ideology of egalitarianism requires that not only should white people *not* be protected by our government, they should be punished. At the same time, the American government relies on the very same white people it is so eager to dispossess for its terrifying economic and military power.

Trump reconciles the contradiction. He invites all Americans to participate in his quest to make the country "great." But because America itself is built on an egalitarian lie and denies the ethnic basis for its own concrete existence, a Trump regime can only delay the inevitable. It might even hasten it, as the anti-white identity politics of the Left will be accelerated under a Trump presidency, as the universities and liberal city governments will practically be in outright rebellion.

Both the American creed of universal classical liberalism and Trump's civic nationalism rely on a white majority. Without explicit white identity politics to safeguard the core population, American can never be great again, let alone greater than it has ever been, as Trump promises.

And who knows? Trump is such a singular actor he might move in that direction.

But regardless of what Trump does or does not do, the only future for the American Right is identity politics. In the more likely scenario Trump doesn't win, it's the end for conservatism. Even if a Republican candidate won the White House, Rubio, Bush, and probably Cruz would promptly work with the Paul Ryan Congress to pass amnesty, thus ensuring conservatism's permanent extinction.

A populist message of national revival built on an America First approach to trade, immigration, and foreign policy can build a long-term winning coalition and give the USA a longer lease on life. As other observers have noted, Trump has tapped into a powerful nationalist force percolating on the Right for many years.

The whole point of the conservative movement is to take this force and funnel it into pointless and defeatist causes. Meanwhile, the concrete interests of the donor class (and the Jewish lobby) are protected. At this point, the Beltway Right is barely bothering to conceal the fact that conservatism is just a scam. The people involved know it is a scam, and the well-meaning lower middle-class goobers babbling about the Constitution are simply functioning as useful idiots.

Even more importantly, absent Trump, it's the end of Americanism. Despite the universalism and claim that there is no "Them" in American conservatism, only whites really believe in Americanism. As demographics change, there is no longer a market for Americanism beyond Glenn Beck-style hucksterism and deeply cynical neocon appeals for "America" to fight Russia. If a billionaire with a massive media megaphone, a celebrity following cultivated over decades, and direct access to millions of Americans can't break this quarantine on nationalism, no one can. The Donald is a *Trump ex machina*, and his movement ends with him. The demographics are such that a project of "nationalist" revival becomes impossible, as well as undesirable, in a matter of years.

So where does that leave whites? Today, whites exist as a group in a negative sense. We are a force of privilege and oppression, a malevolent enemy to the larger world. However, we have no objective existence—"whiteness" is an illusion created by capitalism or an oppressive class system. We therefore have no legitimate group interests.

In contrast, other groups (including Jews) do have legitimate group interests. They also have an objective biologically determined existence, as shown by the Leftist fury directed at Rachel Dolezal. What People of Color lack is agency. Regardless of their numbers, wealth, or state institutions they control, they cannot be racist or sexist because they "lack power." Even Jews masquerade as an "oppressed" group. People of color and Jews are devoid of moral responsibility, mascots for enlightened whites to use to atone for their existence.

To put it another way, whites are in the position of the Third Estate at the beginning of the French Revolution. What are whites in the American system? Everything, in terms of the core culture, the source of political power, and the fount of political legitimacy (as they created the state).

But what are they in the political and social order explicitly? Nothing.

What is our job? To make them something.

And to do that may require a process akin to the French Revolution.

Trump is an opportunity for the System to save itself by giving whites a sense that we still have a place in it. If Trump goes down, it means whites truly have no stake in the existing political order or any legitimate means of political expression. But even if he wins, it's only a temporary reprieve for the United States and for European-Americans. Culturally and historically, whites will never surrender their sense of ownership of the United States, whatever regime rules it. But this is simply nostalgia. The foundation of the entire existing political order is the systematic exploitation, dispossession, and eventual eradication of whites.

For Beltway "conservatives," whites are simply raw material to be used for their ideological agenda or cogs in a cheap labor machine. For the Left, whites are the eternal enemy that unites their Coalition of the Fringes in an everlasting crusade of hatred. Donald Trump promises to stop the "assault" on the historic American nation. He's the last American because he's the last politician who will ever appeal to the core American population, in the name of the old American order, through the old democratic means.

Regardless if he ever wins a single primary, let alone the election, Donald Trump is already a transformational figure. He reveals the System is incapable of saving itself, and European-Americans should plan for what comes next.

Counter-Currents/*North American New Right*,
February 8, 2016

INDEX

This index lists proper names and important concepts. Numbers in bold refer to a whole chapter or section devoted to a particular topic.

ABOUT THE AUTHOR

Gregory Hood is a San Francisco-based writer on politics, religion, and culture. His essays and reviews have been published at Counter-Currents Publishing/*North American New Right*, *Alternative Right*, *Radix Journal,* and *American Renaissance*. This is his first book.